simply

chicken

simply
chicken

100 no fuss recipes for everyday cooking

First published in 2011

LOVE FOOD is an imprint of Parragon Books Ltd

Parragon
Chartist House
15-17 Trim Street
Bath BA1 1HA, UK

ISBN: 978-1-4454-5408-5

Printed in China

Introduction by Linda Doeser
New recipes and additional food styling by Angela Drake
Cover and additional photography by Clive Streeter
Cover and additional food styling by Teresa Goldfinch

This book uses imperial, metric, and US cup measurements. Follow
the same units of measurement throughout; do not mix imperial and
metric. All spoon measurements are level: teaspoons are assumed
to be 5 ml, and tablespoons are assumed to be 15 ml. Unless other-
wise stated, milk is assumed to be whole, eggs are large, individual
vegetables, such as potatoes, are medium, and pepper is freshly
ground black pepper.

The times given are an approximate guide only. Preparation times
differ according to the techniques used by different people and
the cooking times may also vary from those given as a result of
the type of oven used. Optional ingredients, variations, or serving
suggestions have not been included in the calculations.

Recipes using raw or very lightly cooked eggs should be avoided
by infants, the elderly, pregnant women, convalescents, and anyone
with a chronic condition. Pregnant and breast-feeding women are
advised to avoid eating peanuts and peanut products. People with
nut allergies should be aware that some of the prepared ingredients
used in the recipes in this book may contain nuts. Always check the
package before use.

Picture acknowledgments
The publisher would like to thank the following for permission to
reproduce copyright materials: Front cover image: Spicy roast
chicken © Tanya Zouev/Getty Images

Contents

Introduction

If you're an inexperienced cook and want a fail-safe dish, more adventurous and would like to experiment with something different, a busy parent who needs a quick and easy midweek dinner for the family, you've guests coming and you're not sure what to serve, or you just enjoy good food that doesn't take forever to prepare, there's one simple answer. Choose chicken.

Its versatility is almost endless as it goes with the widest possible range of other ingredients, from hot and aromatic spices to rich and creamy sauces and from melt-in-your-mouth Mediterranean vegetables to crisp and refreshing salads. You are guaranteed to find dishes to delight family and friends, whatever their taste. They will also delight you because chicken can be prepared in so many ways—all of them easy. It can be cooked whole or in portions, as drumsticks, thighs, boneless breasts, diced, or ground and may be roasted, casseroled, baked, stir-fried, deep-fried, poached, or broiled. Chicken is perfect for soups, curries, kabobs, wraps, fritters, burgers, pies, pasta sauces, risottos, and salads—the list just goes on.

As chicken is a favorite with children and adults alike, it's ideal for everyday family meals, but it's also perfect for inexpensive and easy entertaining, whether you choose a dish from classic cuisine or try something more unusual and innovative. However, if you have a different main course in mind, why not start the meal with a chicken appetizer? Soup would be just the right thing in the winter, salad in the summer, and pâté, wings, or anything with a dipping sauce at any time of year. Lots of these appetizers also make delicious lunchtime snacks and tempting party treats. In fact, as it is so easily digested and adaptable, chicken is ideal for light bites. Wraps and sandwiches are always popular, but it works well in a wide variety of different quick and easy dishes, such as pizza, burgers, kabobs, and even muffins.

Chicken soup is sometimes reckoned to be the cure for all ills and there may be a grain of truth in this belief in that, together with other light chicken dishes, it's just what the doctor ordered to tempt the appetite when you're recovering from a nasty cold, feeling a bit under the weather, or generally down in the dumps.

Top Tips for Success

• When choosing a fresh chicken look for one with a plump breast and creamy colored skin. The tip of the breast bone should be pliable.

• Store fresh chicken on a plate, covered with wax paper or plastic wrap on the bottom shelf of the refrigerator to avoid cross contamination. Cook within three days of purchase.

• Put frozen chicken, still in its bag, in the freezer as soon as possible after purchasing.

• Thaw frozen birds completely before cooking. Open one end of the bag and put the chicken in a cool place for up to 12 hours. Remove any giblets as soon as you can. The chicken is ready for cooking when the legs are soft and flexible and there are no ice crystals in the cavity.

• Do not rinse chicken under cold running water because, rather than destroying bacteria, this is more likely to spread them.

• Always wash the cutting board, knives, and other utensils thoroughly after preparing raw chicken to remove all traces of bacteria. Wash your hands both before and after handling raw chicken and before touching any other ingredients.

• Test whether chicken is cooked through by inserting the point of a sharp knife in the thickest part of the meat. If the juices run clear, it is ready. If there are any traces of pink, cook for a few minutes more and test again. Check too that the base of the cut is firm and white. The thickest part on a whole bird is the inside of the thigh. If you have a meat thermometer, insert it deep into the thigh meat. The chicken is cooked when the temperature is 175°F/79°C. You can test whether a chicken breast is cooked through by pressing it with your finger; it should feel firm but still springy.

• If you are making stock, either from the carcass of a roasted bird or from a supermarket stew pack, don't add salt as it may become very concentrated during cooking and spoil the flavor. If using stock cubes or powder, check the salt content listed on the label before buying and try to find a brand that is low in salt.

• Chicken is always leaner than red meat but if you are concerned about lowering fat and cholesterol levels in the family diet, remove the skin before cooking, as most of the fat is located just beneath it.

Snack Attack

chicken noodle soup

SERVES 4

2 skinless, boneless chicken breasts

5 cups water or chicken stock

3 carrots, cut into ¼-inch/5-mm slices

3 oz/85 g vermicelli (or other fine noodles)

salt and pepper

fresh tarragon leaves, to garnish

1 Place the chicken breasts in a large saucepan, add the water, and bring to a simmer. Cook for 25–30 minutes. Skim any foam from the surface, if necessary. Remove the chicken from the liquid and keep warm.

2 Continue to simmer the liquid, add the carrots and vermicelli, and cook for 4–5 minutes.

3 Thinly slice or shred the chicken breasts and divide among four warmed bowls.

4 Season the soup to taste with salt and pepper and pour over the chicken. Garnish with tarragon leaves and serve immediately.

chicken & rice soup

SERVES 4

6¾ cups chicken stock

2 small carrots, very thinly sliced

1 celery stalk, finely diced

1 baby leek, halved lengthwise and thinly sliced

4 oz/115 g young green peas, thawed if frozen

1 cup cooked rice

5½ oz/150 g cooked chicken, sliced

2 tsp chopped fresh tarragon

1 tbsp chopped fresh flat-leaf parsley, plus extra sprigs to garnish

salt and pepper

1 Put the stock in a large saucepan and add the carrots, celery, and leek. Bring to a boil, reduce the heat to low, and simmer gently, partially covered, for 10 minutes.

2 Stir in the peas, rice, and chicken, and continue cooking for an additional 10–15 minutes, or until the vegetables are tender.

3 Add the chopped tarragon and parsley, then taste and adjust the seasoning, adding salt and pepper if needed.

4 Ladle the soup into warmed serving bowls, garnish with parsley sprigs, and serve immediately.

chicken & potato soup with bacon

SERVES 4

1 tbsp butter

2 garlic cloves, chopped

1 onion, sliced

9 oz/250 g smoked lean bacon, chopped

2 large leeks, sliced

2 tbsp all-purpose flour

4 cups chicken stock

1 lb 12 oz/800 g potatoes, chopped

7 oz/200 g skinless boneless chicken breasts, chopped

4 tbsp heavy cream

salt and pepper

broiled bacon and fresh flat-leaf parsley sprigs, to garnish

1 Melt the butter in a large pan over medium heat. Add the garlic and onion, and cook, stirring, for 3 minutes, until slightly softened. Add the chopped bacon and leeks, and cook for another 3 minutes, stirring.

2 In a bowl, mix the flour with enough of the stock to make a smooth paste and stir it into the pan. Cook, stirring, for 2 minutes.

3 Pour in the remaining stock, then add the potatoes and chicken. Season to taste with salt and pepper. Bring to a boil, then reduce the heat and simmer for 25 minutes, until the chicken and potatoes are tender and cooked through.

4 Stir in the cream and cook for another 2 minutes, then remove from the heat and ladle into warmed serving bowls. Garnish with broiled bacon and parsley sprigs and serve immediately.

thai chicken soup

SERVES 6

1 tbsp sesame oil or chili oil

2 garlic cloves, chopped

2 scallions, sliced

1 leek, finely sliced

1 tbsp grated fresh ginger

1 red chile, seeded and finely chopped

12 oz/350 g skinless, boneless chicken breasts, cut into strips

scant 3½ cups chicken stock

2 tbsp rice wine

1 tbsp chopped lemongrass

6 kaffir lime leaves, finely shredded

7 oz/200 g fine egg noodles

salt and pepper

1 Heat the oil in a wok or large pan. Add the garlic and cook over medium heat, stirring, for 1 minute. Add the scallions, leek, ginger, and chile, and cook, stirring, for an additional 3 minutes.

2 Add the chicken, stock, and rice wine, bring to a boil, reduce the heat, and simmer for 20 minutes. Stir in the lemongrass and lime leaves.

3 Bring a separate pan of water to a boil and add the noodles. Cook for 3 minutes, or according to the packet instructions, then drain well and add to the soup. Season to taste with salt and pepper. Cook for another 2 minutes. Remove from the heat, ladle into warmed serving bowls, and serve immediately.

Step 1

Step 2

Step 3

chicken & broccoli soup

SERVES 4–6

8 oz/225 g head of broccoli

4 tbsp unsalted butter

1 onion, chopped

2 tbsp basmati rice

8 oz/225 g skinless, boneless chicken breasts, cut into thin slivers

scant ¼ cup all-purpose whole wheat flour

1¼ cups milk

2 cups chicken stock

generous ⅓ cup corn kernels

salt and pepper

1 Break the broccoli into small florets and cook in a pan of lightly salted boiling water for 3 minutes. Drain then plunge into cold water and set aside.

2 Melt the butter in a pan over medium heat, add the onion, rice, and chicken, and cook, stirring frequently, for 5 minutes.

3 Remove the pan from the heat and stir in the flour. Return to the heat and cook for 2 minutes, stirring constantly. Stir in the milk and then the stock. Bring to a boil, stirring constantly, then reduce the heat and let simmer for 10 minutes.

4 Drain the broccoli and add to the pan with the corn. Taste and adjust the seasoning, adding salt and pepper if needed. Let simmer for 5 minutes, or until the rice is tender. Ladle into warmed bowls and serve immediately.

cream of chicken soup

SERVES 4

3 tbsp butter

4 shallots, chopped

1 leek, sliced

1 lb/450 g skinless, boneless chicken breasts, chopped

2½ cups chicken stock

1 tbsp chopped fresh parsley

1 tbsp chopped fresh thyme, plus extra sprigs to garnish

¾ cup heavy cream

salt and pepper

1 Melt the butter in a large pan over medium heat. Add the shallots and cook, stirring, for 3 minutes, until slightly softened. Add the leek and cook, stirring, for an additional 5 minutes.

2 Add the chicken, stock, and chopped herbs, and season to taste with salt and pepper. Bring to a boil, then reduce the heat and simmer for 25 minutes, until the chicken is tender and cooked through. Remove from the heat and let cool for 10 minutes.

3 Transfer the soup into a food processor or blender and process until smooth (you may need to do this in batches). Return the soup to the rinsed-out pan and warm over low heat for 5 minutes.

4 Stir in the cream and cook for another 2 minutes, then remove from the heat and ladle into warmed serving bowls. Garnish with thyme sprigs and serve immediately.

chicken soup with matzo balls

SERVES 6

2 chicken quarters

11 cups vegetable stock

2 onions, chopped

2 celery stalks, chopped

2 carrots, chopped

2 tomatoes, peeled and chopped

2 fresh parsley sprigs, plus chopped parsley to garnish

2 oz/55 g vermicelli

salt and pepper

matzo balls

4 tbsp butter

½ onion, grated

1 egg

1 egg yolk

1 tbsp finely chopped fresh parsley

1 tbsp water

2 cups crushed matzo crackers

salt and pepper

1 First, make the matzo balls. Melt 1 tbsp of the butter in a small skillet. Add the grated onion and cook over low heat, stirring occasionally, for 5 minutes, until softened. Remove from the heat and let cool.

2 Beat the remaining butter in a bowl until fluffy, then gradually beat in the egg and egg yolk. Add the finely chopped parsley and fried onion. Season to taste with salt and pepper, and mix well, then beat in the water. Mix in the matzo crumbs until thoroughly incorporated. Cover and let rest in the refrigerator for 30 minutes.

3 Meanwhile, put the chicken into a large pan and pour in the vegetable stock. Bring to a boil over low–medium heat, skimming off the foam that rises to the surface. Simmer for 15 minutes.

4 Add the chopped onion, celery, carrots, tomatoes, and parsley sprigs and season to taste with salt and pepper. Reduce the heat, cover, and simmer for 50–60 minutes, until the chicken is cooked through and tender. Meanwhile, shape the matzo mixture into 18 balls.

5 Strain the soup into a clean pan, reserving the chicken quarters. Remove and discard the skin and bones and cut the meat into bite-size pieces. Add the chicken, vermicelli, and matzo balls to the pan, cover, and simmer gently for 20–30 minutes. Ladle into warmed bowls, garnish with chopped parsley and serve immediately.

chicken caesar salad

SERVES 4

3 tbsp sunflower oil

2 thick slices of white bread, cubed

3 skinless, boneless chicken breasts, about 5 oz/140 g each

2 small heads of romaine lettuce, coarsely chopped

2 tbsp Parmesan cheese shavings

salt and pepper

dressing

1 garlic clove, crushed

2 canned anchovy fillets, drained and finely chopped

5 tbsp light olive oil

2 tbsp white wine vinegar

2 tbsp mayonnaise

2 tbsp freshly grated Parmesan cheese

salt and pepper

1 Preheat the oven to 400°F/200°C. Put 2 tablespoons of the sunflower oil in a bowl, add the bread, and toss to coat in the oil. Spread out on a baking sheet, season well with salt and pepper, and bake in the preheated oven for 10 minutes, until crisp and golden brown.

2 Meanwhile, brush the chicken breasts with the remaining sunflower oil and season to taste with salt and pepper. Cook on a preheated cast-iron skillet for 8–10 minutes on each side, until the chicken is tender and the juices run clear when a sharp knife is inserted into the thickest part of the meat.

3 To make the dressing, put all the ingredients in a small bowl and mix thoroughly until smooth and creamy.

4 Slice the hot cooked chicken and toss lightly with the lettuce and croutons. Divide the salad among four serving bowls and drizzle with the dressing. Sprinkle with the Parmesan cheese shavings and serve immediately.

Step 1

Step 2

Step 3

waldorf chicken salad

1 lb 2 oz/500 g red dessert apples, diced

3 tbsp fresh lemon juice

⅔ cup light mayonnaise

1 head of celery

4 shallots, sliced

1 garlic clove, finely chopped

¾ cup chopped walnuts, chopped, plus extra to garnish

1 lb 2 oz/500 g cooked chicken, cubed

1 head of romaine lettuce

pepper

1 Place the apples in a large bowl with the lemon juice and 1 tablespoon of the mayonnaise. Mix together well. Let stand for 40 minutes.

2 Using a sharp knife, slice the celery very thinly. Add the celery, shallots, garlic, and walnuts to the apples and mix together. Stir in the remaining mayonnaise and mix thoroughly.

3 Add the chicken, season to taste with pepper, and mix with the other ingredients.

4 Line four serving dishes with the lettuce leaves. Divide the chicken salad among the dishes, garnish with walnuts and serve immediately.

chicken, cheese & arugula salad

SERVES 4

5½ oz/150 g arugula leaves

2 celery stalks, sliced

½ cucumber, sliced

2 scallions, sliced

2 tbsp chopped fresh parsley

¼ cup chopped walnuts

12 oz/350 g cold roast chicken, sliced

4½ oz/125 g bleu cheese, cubed

handful of seedless red grapes, cut in half (optional)

salt and pepper

dressing

2 tbsp olive oil

1 tbsp sherry vinegar

1 tsp whole grain mustard

1 tbsp chopped fresh mixed herbs

1 Put the arugula leaves into a large bowl. Add the celery, cucumber, scallions, parsley, and walnuts, and mix together well. Transfer to a large serving dish.

2 Arrange the chicken slices over the salad, then scatter over the bleu cheese. Add the grapes, if using. Season well with salt and pepper.

3 To make the dressing, put all the ingredients into a screw-top jar and shake well. Alternatively, put them into a bowl and mix together well. Drizzle the dressing over the salad, toss gently, and serve immediately.

cajun chicken salad

SERVES 4

4 skinless, boneless chicken breasts, about 5 oz/140 g each

4 tsp Cajun seasoning

2 tsp corn oil

1 ripe mango, peeled, pitted, and cut into thick slices

7 oz/200 g mixed salad greens

1 red onion, halved and thinly sliced

6 oz/175 g cooked beet, diced

3 oz/85 g radishes, sliced

generous ⅜ cup walnut halves

2 tbsp sesame seeds

dressing

4 tbsp walnut oil

1–2 tsp whole grain mustard

1 tbsp lemon juice

salt and pepper

1 Make three diagonal slashes across each chicken breast. Put the chicken into a shallow dish and sprinkle all over with the Cajun seasoning. Cover and let chill in the refrigerator for 30 minutes.

2 When ready to cook, brush a stove-top grill pan with the corn oil. Heat over high heat until very hot and a few drops of water sprinkled into the pan sizzle immediately. Add the chicken and cook for 7–8 minutes on each side, or until the chicken is tender and the juices run clear when a sharp knife is inserted into the thickest part of the meat. Remove the chicken from the pan and set aside.

3 Add the mango slices to the pan and cook for 2 minutes on each side. Remove and set aside.

4 Meanwhile, arrange the salad greens in a serving dish and sprinkle over the onion, beet, radishes, and walnuts.

5 To make the dressing, put all the ingredients into a screw-top jar and shake well. Alternatively, put them in a bowl and mix together well. Drizzle the dressing over the salad, toss gently and sprinkle with the sesame seeds.

6 Cut the chicken into thick slices. Arrange the mango and the salad on a serving plate and top with the chicken breast and a few of the salad greens.

smoked chicken & cranberry salad

SERVES 4

1 smoked chicken, weighing 3 lb/1.3 kg

scant 1 cup dried cranberries

2 tbsp apple juice or water

7 oz/200 g sugar snap peas

2 ripe avocados

juice of ½ lemon

4 lettuce hearts

1 bunch of watercress

2 oz/55 g arugula

½ cup chopped walnuts, (optional)

dressing

2 tbsp olive oil

1 tbsp walnut oil

2 tbsp lemon juice

1 tbsp chopped fresh mixed herbs, such as parsley and lemon thyme

salt and pepper

1 Carve the chicken carefully, slicing the white meat. Divide the legs into thighs and drumsticks, and trim the wings. Cover with plastic wrap and chill in the refrigerator.

2 Put the cranberries in a bowl. Stir in the apple juice, then cover with plastic wrap and let soak for 30 minutes.

3 Meanwhile, blanch the sugar snap peas, then refresh under cold running water and drain.

4 Peel, pit, and slice the avocados, and toss in the lemon juice to prevent discoloration.

5 Separate the lettuce hearts and arrange on serving plates with the avocados, sugar snap peas, watercress, arugula, and chicken.

6 To make the dressing, put all the ingredients into a screw-top jar and shake well. Alternatively, put them in a bowl and mix together well.

7 Drain the cranberries and mix them with the dressing, then pour over the salad. Scatter the walnuts, if using, over the salad and serve immediately.

Step 2

Step 3

Step 6

chicken & spinach salad

SERVES 4

3 celery stalks, thinly sliced

½ cucumber, thinly sliced

2 scallions, thinly sliced

9 oz/250 g baby spinach leaves

3 tbsp chopped fresh flat-leaf parsley

12 oz/350 g roast chicken, thinly sliced

smoked almonds, to garnish

dressing

1-inch/2.5-cm piece of fresh ginger, finely grated

3 tbsp olive oil

1 tbsp white wine vinegar

1 tbsp honey

½ tsp ground cinnamon

salt and pepper

1 Toss the celery, cucumber, and scallions in a large bowl with the spinach and parsley.

2 Transfer to serving plates and arrange the chicken on top of the salad.

3 To make the dressing, put all the ingredients into a screw-top jar and shake well. Alternatively, put them in a bowl and mix together well. Pour the dressing over the salad, garnish with a few smoked almonds and serve immediately.

coronation chicken

SERVES 6

4 tbsp olive oil

2 lb/900 g skinless, boneless chicken, diced

⅔ cup diced, rindless, smoked bacon,

12 shallots

2 garlic cloves, finely chopped

1 tbsp mild curry powder

1¼ cups mayonnaise

1 tbsp honey

1 tbsp chopped fresh flat-leaf parsley

pepper

½ cup seedless white grapes, quartered

cold saffron rice, to serve

1 Heat the oil in a large skillet and add the chicken, bacon, shallots, garlic, and curry powder. Cook slowly, stirring, for about 15 minutes, until the chicken is cooked through.

2 Spoon the mixture into a large bowl. Allow to cool completely, then season to taste with pepper.

3 Blend the mayonnaise with the honey, then add the parsley. Toss the chicken mixture in the mayonnaise mixture.

4 Spoon the chicken mixture into a serving dish and scatter over the grapes. Serve immediately with cold saffron rice.

layered chicken salad

SERVES 4

1 lb 10 oz/750 g new potatoes, scrubbed

1 red bell pepper, halved and seeded

1 green bell pepper, halved and seeded

2 small zucchini, sliced

1 small onion, thinly sliced

3 tomatoes, sliced

12 oz/350 g cold roast chicken, sliced

salt

snipped fresh chives, to garnish

dressing

⅔ cup plain yogurt

3 tbsp mayonnaise

1 tbsp snipped fresh chives

salt and pepper

1 Put the potatoes into a large pan, add just enough cold water to cover, and bring to a boil. Reduce the heat, cover, and simmer for 15–20 minutes, until tender.

2 Meanwhile, preheat the broiler to high. Place the bell pepper halves, skin side up, under the preheated broiler and cook until the skins blacken and begin to char.

3 Remove the bell peppers with tongs, place in a bowl, and cover with plastic wrap. Set aside until cool enough to handle, then peel off the skins and slice the flesh.

4 Bring a small pan of lightly salted water to a boil. Add the zucchini, bring back to a boil, reduce the heat, and simmer for 3 minutes. Drain, rinse under cold running water, and drain again. Set aside.

5 To make the dressing, whisk together the yogurt, mayonnaise, and chopped chives in a small bowl until well blended. Season to taste with salt and pepper.

6 When the potatoes are tender, drain, cool, and slice them. Divide the potato slices equally among four plates and drizzle the dressing over them.

7 Top each plate with one quarter of the bell pepper and zucchini slices. Layer one quarter of the onion and tomato slices, then the sliced chicken, on top of each serving. Garnish with chopped chives and serve immediately.

chicken crostini

SERVES 4

12 slices of French bread or country bread

4 tbsp olive oil

2 garlic cloves, chopped

2 tbsp finely chopped fresh oregano, plus extra to garnish

3½ oz/100 g cold roast chicken, cut into small, thin slices

4 tomatoes, sliced

12 thin slices of goat cheese

12 black olives, pitted and chopped

salt and pepper

1 Preheat the broiler to medium. Put the bread under the broiler and lightly toast on both sides.

2 Meanwhile, pour the oil into a bowl and add the garlic and oregano. Season with salt and pepper and mix well. Remove the toasted bread slices from the broiler and brush them on one side only with a little of the oil mixture.

3 Preheat the oven to 350°F/180°C. Place the bread slices, oiled sides up, on a cookie sheet. Put some of the sliced chicken on top of each one, followed by a slice of tomato.

4 Divide the slices of goat cheese among the bread slices, then top with the olives.

5 Drizzle over the remaining oil mixture and transfer to the preheated oven. Bake for about 5 minutes, or until the cheese is golden and starting to melt. Garnish with oregano and serve immediately.

Step 1

Step 2

Step 3

chicken liver pâté

SERVES 4–6

1 cup butter

8 oz/225 g trimmed chicken livers, thawed if frozen

2 tbsp Marsala wine or brandy

1½ tsp chopped fresh sage

1 garlic clove, coarsely chopped

⅔ cup heavy cream

salt and pepper

fresh bay leaves or sage leaves, to garnish

crackers, to serve

1 Melt 3 tablespoons of the butter in a large, heavy-bottom skillet. Add the chicken livers and cook over medium heat for about 4 minutes on each side. They should be browned on the outside but still pink in the middle. Transfer to a food processor and process until finely chopped.

2 Stir the Marsala or brandy into the skillet, scraping up any sediment with a wooden spoon, then add to the food processor with the sage, garlic, and ½ cup of the remaining butter. Process until smooth. Add the cream, season to taste with salt and pepper, and process until thoroughly combined and smooth. Spoon the pâté into a serving dish or individual dishes, level the surface, and let cool completely.

3 Melt the remaining butter, then spoon it over the surface of the pâté. Decorate with bay leaves and let cool slightly, then let chill in the refrigerator. Serve with crackers.

chicken livers in red wine

SERVES 4

3 tbsp lemon-flavored oil

2 garlic cloves, finely chopped

9 oz/250 g trimmed chicken livers, thawed if frozen

4 tbsp red wine

1 tbsp chopped fresh thyme, plus extra sprigs to garnish

salt and pepper

arugula leaves, to serve

1 Heat the oil in a skillet. Add the garlic and cook, stirring, over medium heat for 2 minutes. Add the chicken livers, wine, and chopped thyme. Season to taste with salt and pepper and cook for 3 minutes.

2 Meanwhile, arrange the arugula in serving dishes. Remove the pan from the heat and spoon the chicken livers over the arugula. Pour over the cooking juices, then garnish with thyme sprigs and serve immediately.

sesame chicken wings

MAKES 24

4 tbsp olive oil, plus extra for brushing

juice and finely grated rind of 2 lemons

1 tbsp light brown sugar

pinch of cayenne pepper, or to taste

24 chicken wings

2 tbsp sesame seeds

salt and pepper

1 Preheat the oven to 400°F/200°C. Line a roasting pan with foil, then put a broiler rack in the pan.

2 Put the oil in a bowl, add the lemon juice and rind, sugar, cayenne pepper, and salt and pepper to taste and stir until the sugar has dissolved. Add the chicken wings and use your hands to coat well with the marinade. At this point, you can cook the wings immediately or cover and let marinate in the refrigerator for several hours.

3 Generously brush the broiler rack with oil. Arrange the wings on the rack in a single layer and sprinkle with the sesame seeds. If your broiler rack isn't large enough to hold all the wings, cook in batches. Roast in the preheated oven for 25–30 minutes, until the juices run clear when a sharp knife is inserted into the thickest part of the meat, and the skin is crisp. Drain on paper towels and let cool before serving.

oven-fried chicken wings

SERVES 4

12 chicken wings

1 egg

½ cup milk

4 heaping tbsp all-purpose flour

1 tsp paprika

2 cups fresh breadcrumbs

2 oz/55 g butter, melted

salt and pepper

1 Preheat the oven to 425°F/220°C. Cut each of the chicken wings into three pieces. Discard the bony tip. Beat the egg with the milk in a shallow dish. Combine the flour, paprika, and salt and pepper to taste in a separate shallow dish. Place the breadcrumbs in another shallow dish.

2 Dip the chicken pieces into the seasoned flour and coat first in the egg mixture, allowing any excess to drip back into the dish, then in the breadcrumbs.

3 Pour the melted butter into a shallow roasting pan that is large enough to hold all the chicken pieces in a single layer. Arrange the chicken, skin side down, in the pan and bake in the preheated oven for 10 minutes. Turn and bake for an additional 10 minutes, or until golden brown and the juices run clear when a sharp knife is inserted into the thickest part of the meat.

4 Remove the chicken from the pan and arrange on a large platter. Serve hot or at room temperature.

Step 1

Step 2

Step 3

spicy chicken wings

SERVES 4

2 lb/900 g chicken wings

lime wedges, to serve

marinade

11 garlic cloves, finely chopped

juice of 2 limes

juice of 1 orange

2 tbsp tequila

1 tbsp mild chili powder

2 dried chipotle chiles, soaked in hot water for 15 minutes, drained, and pureed

2 tbsp vegetable oil

1 tsp sugar

¼ tsp ground allspice

pinch of ground cinnamon

pinch of ground cumin

pinch of dried oregano

1 Cut each of the chicken wings into two pieces at the joint.

2 Place the chicken pieces in a nonmetallic dish and add all the marinade ingredients. Toss well to coat, then cover and let marinate in the refrigerator for at least 3 hours, or overnight.

3 Preheat the broiler or a ridged grill pan. Cook the chicken wings, turning occasionally, for 15–20 minutes, or until the juices run clear when a sharp knife is inserted into the thickest part of the meat and the skin is crisp. Serve immediately with lime wedges for squeezing over.

chicken balls with dipping sauce

SERVES 4

2 large skinless, boneless chicken breasts

3 tbsp vegetable oil

2 shallots, finely chopped

½ celery stalk, finely chopped

1 garlic clove, crushed

2 tbsp light soy sauce

1 small egg

1 bunch of scallions

salt and pepper

dipping sauce

3 tbsp dark soy sauce

1 tbsp rice wine

1 tsp sesame seeds

1 Cut the chicken into ¾-inch/2-cm pieces. Heat half of the oil in a skillet and stir-fry the chicken over high heat for 2–3 minutes, until golden. Remove from the skillet with a slotted spoon and set aside.

2 Add the shallots, celery, and garlic to the skillet and stir-fry for 1–2 minutes, until softened.

3 Place the chicken and the shallot mixture in a food processor and process until finely ground. Add 1 tablespoon of the light soy sauce and just enough of the egg to make a fairly firm mixture. Season to taste with salt and pepper.

4 Make the dipping sauce by mixing together the dark soy sauce, rice wine, and sesame seeds in a small serving bowl and set aside.

5 Shape the chicken mixture into 16 walnut-size balls. Heat the remaining oil in the skillet and stir-fry the chicken balls in small batches for 4–5 minutes, until golden brown. Drain on paper towels.

6 Add the scallions to the skillet and stir-fry for 1–2 minutes, until they begin to soften, then stir in the remaining light soy sauce. Serve the chicken balls with the stir-fried scallions and the dipping sauce.

chicken & apple balls

MAKES 20

1 dessert apple, peeled, cored, and grated

2 skinless, boneless chicken breasts, cut into chunks

½ red onion, minced

1 tbsp minced fresh parsley

scant 1 cup fresh whole wheat breadcrumbs

1 tbsp concentrated chicken stock

whole wheat flour, for coating

peanut oil, for pan-frying

1 Spread the apple out on a clean dish towel and press out all the excess moisture.

2 Put the chicken, apple, onion, parsley, breadcrumbs, and stock in a food processor or blender and blend briefly until well combined.

3 Spread the flour out on a plate. Divide the mixture into 20 portions, shape each portion into a ball, and roll in the flour.

4 Heat enough oil for shallow-frying in a nonstick skillet over medium heat and cook the balls for 5–8 minutes, or until golden brown all over and cooked through. Remove and drain on paper towels. Serve hot or cold.

chicken satay

SERVES 4

4 tbsp smooth peanut butter

generous ⅓ cup soy sauce

4 skinless, boneless chicken breasts, cut into thin strips

lemon wedges and cooked rice, to serve

1 Preheat the broiler. Mix the peanut butter and soy sauce together in a bowl until smooth. Stir in the chicken strips, tossing well to coat in the mixture.

2 Thread the chicken strips onto four metal or presoaked, wooden skewers and cook under the preheated broiler for about 5 minutes on each side, or until cooked through. Serve immediately with freshly cooked rice and lemon wedges for squeezing over.

VARIATION
For a spicy peanut sauce to accompany the skewers, place 2 tbsp peanut butter, scant 1 cup of coconut cream, 2 tsp Thai red curry paste, 1 tbsp Thai fish sauce, and 1 tbsp brown sugar in a pan. Heat gently, stirring constantly, to form a smooth sauce.

2

Light
Bites

baked potatoes with chicken

SERVES 4

4 large baking potatoes

9 oz/250 g cooked chicken, cubed

4 scallions, thickly sliced

1 cup soft cheese

pepper

mixed salad, to serve

1 Preheat the oven to 400°F/200°C. Prick the potatoes all over with a fork. Bake in the preheated oven for about 60 minutes, or until tender. Alternatively, cook in a microwave on high power for 12–15 minutes.

2 Place the chicken and scallions in a bowl, add the soft cheese and mix together well.

3 Cut a cross into the top of each potato and squeeze slightly apart. Spoon the chicken filling into the potatoes and season to taste with pepper. Serve immediately with a mixed salad.

chicken & cheese toasts

SERVES 4

2 cups grated crumbly cheese

1⅓ cups cooked chicken, shredded

1 tbsp butter

1 tbsp Worcestershire sauce

1 tsp dry mustard

2 tsp all-purpose flour

4 tbsp mild beer

4 slices of bread

salt and pepper

cherry tomatoes, to serve

1 Place the cheese, chicken, butter, Worcestershire sauce, dry mustard, flour, and beer in a small pan. Mix all the ingredients together, then season to taste with salt and pepper.

2 Gently bring the mixture to a boil and remove from the heat immediately. Using a wooden spoon, beat until the mixture becomes creamy in texture. Let it cool.

3 Preheat the broiler. Toast the bread on both sides and spread with the chicken mixture.

4 Place back under a hot broiler and broil until bubbling and golden brown. Serve with cherry tomatoes.

open chicken sandwiches

SERVES 6

3 hard-boiled eggs

2 tbsp butter, softened

2 tbsp mustard

1 tsp anchovy extract

2 cups grated cheddar cheese

3 cooked skinless, boneless chicken breasts, diced

6 thick slices of rustic bread, buttered

pepper

sliced tomato and cucumber, to serve

1 Cut the hard-boiled eggs in half lengthwise and separate the yolks and whites. Mash the egg yolks and chop the whites.

2 In a large bowl, mix the egg yolks and whites with the butter, mustard, and anchovy extract. Season to taste with pepper.

3 Mix in the cheese and chicken, then spread the mixture on the bread.

4 Arrange the tomato and cucumber slices on top and serve immediately.

smoked chicken & ham focaccia

SERVES 2–4

1 thick focaccia loaf

handful of fresh basil leaves

2 small zucchini, coarsely shredded

6 wafer-thin slices of smoked chicken

6 wafer-thin slices of cooked ham

8 oz/225 g Taleggio cheese, cut into strips

freshly grated nutmeg (optional)

cherry tomatoes and salad leaves, to serve

1 Preheat a grill pan under the broiler until both broiler and grill pan are hot. If you do not have a grill pan, heat a heavy baking sheet or roasting pan instead. Slice the focaccia in half horizontally and cut the top half lengthwise into strips.

2 Cover the bottom half of the focaccia with an even layer of the grated zucchini, then cover with the basil leaves. Cover this with the chicken and ham. Lay the strips of focaccia on top, placing strips of cheese between them. Sprinkle with a little nutmeg, if using.

3 Place the assembled bread on the preheated grill pan and cook under the broiler, well away from the heat, for about 5 minutes, until the cheese has melted, and the top of the bread is browned. Cut the focaccia into four pieces and serve immediately with cherry tomatoes and salad leaves.

Step 1

Step 2

Step 2

chicken stuffed baguette

SERVES 2

1 garlic clove, halved

1 large baguette stick, sliced lengthwise

½ cup olive oil

2 oz/55 g cold roast chicken, thinly sliced

fresh basil leaves

2 large tomatoes, sliced

¾ oz/20 g canned anchovy fillets, drained

8 large pitted black olives, chopped

pepper

1 Rub the garlic over the insides of the baguette and sprinkle with the oil.

2 Arrange the chicken on top of the bread. Scatter the basil leaves over the chicken. Place the tomatoes and anchovies on top of the chicken.

3 Scatter with the black olives, and season with plenty of pepper. Sandwich the baguette back together and wrap tightly in foil until required. Cut into slices to serve.

chicken wraps

SERVES 4

⅔ **cup plain yogurt**

1 tbsp whole grain mustard

10 oz/280 g cooked skinless, boneless chicken breasts, diced

5 oz/140 g iceberg lettuce, finely shredded

3 oz/85 g cucumber, thinly sliced

2 celery stalks, sliced

½ **cup black seedless grapes, halved**

4 large flour tortillas

pepper

1 Combine the yogurt and mustard in a bowl and season to taste with pepper. Stir in the chicken and toss until thoroughly coated.

2 Put the lettuce, cucumber, celery, and grapes into a separate bowl and mix well.

3 Fold a tortilla in half and in half again to make a cone that is easy to hold. Half-fill the tortilla pocket with a quarter of the salad mixture and top with a quarter of the chicken mixture. Repeat with the remaining tortillas, salad, and chicken. Serve immediately.

caesar chicken wraps

MAKES 4

2 skinless, boneless chicken breasts

1 tbsp olive oil

2 eggs

4 x large sun-dried tomato flour tortillas

4 Boston lettuce leaves, washed

4 white anchovies

2 tbsp freshly grated Parmesan cheese

salt and pepper

caesar dressing

3 tbsp mayonnaise

1 tbsp water

½ tbsp white wine vinegar

salt and pepper

1 Preheat the oven to 400°F/200°C. Place the chicken breasts on a nonstick baking sheet. Rub the chicken with the oil, and season to taste with salt and pepper. Place in the preheated oven and cook for 20 minutes or until tender and the juices run clear when a sharp knife is inserted into the thickest part of the meat. Remove from the oven and let cool.

2 Bring a small saucepan of water to a boil and add the eggs. Cook for 9 minutes, then cool under cold running water. Once cooled, shell and roughly chop the eggs. Shred the chicken and combine with the chopped egg.

3 To make the dressing, put all the ingredients into a screw-top jar and shake well. Alternatively, put them in a bowl and mix together well. Combine with the chicken and egg, then set aside.

4 Heat a nonstick skillet or griddle pan, then add the tortillas, one at a time, and warm for 10 seconds on each side.

5 Place a lettuce leaf in the center of each tortilla, then top with the chicken mixture, anchovies, and cheese. Roll up each filled tortilla and cut crossways into small slices. Serve immediately.

chicken quesadillas

SERVES 4

3–4 tbsp sunflower oil

1 red onion, thinly sliced

14 oz/400 g skinless, boneless chicken breasts, finely chopped

1 yellow bell pepper, seeded and thinly sliced

1 tsp chili powder

8 flour tortillas

½ cup mild salsa

2 cups grated cheddar cheese

4 tbsp chopped fresh cilantro

salt and pepper

to serve

sour cream

guacamole

lime wedges

1 Heat 1 tablespoon of the oil in a skillet and cook the onion for 5 minutes, until softened. Add the chicken and bell pepper and cook over medium–high heat, stirring frequently, for 10–12 minutes, until the chicken is golden brown and cooked through. Stir in the chili powder and season to taste with salt and pepper.

2 Take one tortilla and spread with 2 tablespoons of the salsa leaving a ½-inch/1-cm border around the edge of the tortilla. Spread a quarter of the chicken mixture on top and sprinkle with a quarter of the grated cheese and cilantro. Put a second tortilla on top, pressing down gently. Repeat with the remaining ingredients to make four quesadillas in total.

3 Heat a little of the remaining oil in a large skillet and cook the quesadillas, one at a time, for 3–4 minutes on each side, until crisp and lightly browned, adding more oil as necessary. Cut the quesadillas into quarters and serve immediately with sour cream, guacamole, and lime wedges.

Step
1

Step
1

Step
2

chicken fajitas

SERVES 4

3 tbsp olive oil

3 tbsp maple syrup or honey

1 tbsp red wine vinegar

2 garlic cloves, crushed

2 tsp dried oregano

1–2 tsp dried chile flakes

4 skinless, boneless chicken breasts

2 red bell peppers, seeded and cut into 1-inch/ 2.5-cm strips

8 flour tortillas

salt and pepper

shredded lettuce, to serve

1 Place the oil, maple syrup, vinegar, garlic, oregano, chile flakes, and salt and pepper to taste in a large, shallow dish and mix together.

2 Slice the chicken across the grain into slices 1 inch/ 2.5 cm thick. Toss in the marinade until well coated. Cover and let marinate in the refrigerator for 2–3 hours, turning occasionally.

3 Heat a grill pan until hot. Lift the chicken slices from the marinade with a slotted spoon, discarding the marinade. Place the chicken on the grill pan, and cook over medium–high heat for 3–4 minutes on each side, or until cooked through. Transfer the chicken to a plate and keep warm.

4 Add the bell peppers, skin-side down, to the grill pan and cook for 2 minutes on each side. Transfer to the plate.

5 Heat a nonstick skillet or griddle pan, then add the tortillas, one at a time, and warm for 10 seconds on each side. Divide the chicken and peppers among the tortillas. Top with a little shredded lettuce, wrap and serve immediately.

chicken & chile enchiladas

SERVES 4

corn oil, for brushing

5 fresh hot green chiles, such as jalapeño, seeded and chopped

1 Spanish onion, chopped

2 garlic cloves, chopped

2 tbsp chopped fresh cilantro

2 tbsp lime juice

½ cup chicken stock

2 beefsteak tomatoes, peeled, seeded, and chopped

pinch of sugar

12 oz/350 g cooked chicken, shredded

¾ cup cheddar cheese, grated

2 tsp chopped fresh oregano

8 corn or flour tortillas

salt

1 Preheat the oven to 350°F/180°C. Brush a large, ovenproof dish with oil. Place two-thirds of the chiles, the onion, garlic, cilantro, lime juice, stock, tomatoes, and sugar in a food processor and pulse to a purée. Scrape into a pan and let simmer over medium heat for 10 minutes, until thickened.

2 Mix together the remaining chiles, the chicken, ½ cup of the cheese and the oregano. Season to taste with salt and stir in half the sauce.

3 Heat a nonstick skillet or griddle pan, then add the tortillas, one at a time, and warm for 10 seconds on each side. Divide the chicken mixture among the tortillas, spooning it along the centers, then roll up and place, seam side down, in the prepared dish.

4 Pour the remaining sauce over the enchiladas and sprinkle with the remaining cheese. Bake in the preheated oven for 20 minutes, until the cheese is golden and bubbling. Serve immediately.

deep dish chicken feast pizza

SERVES 2–4

4 tbsp olive oil, plus extra for brushing

⅓ cup diced smoked bacon

1 onion, finely chopped

10 oz/280 g skinless, boneless chicken breasts, cut into strips

1 tsp chopped fresh tarragon

4 oz/115 g sliced smoked chicken, cut into strips

1 x 15-inch/38-cm store-bought pizza base

pinch of dried oregano

1¼ cups grated mozzarella cheese

1 Heat 2 tablespoons of the oil in a skillet. Add the bacon and onion and cook over low heat, stirring occasionally, for 5 minutes, until softened. Add the fresh chicken, increase the heat to medium, and stir-fry for 4–5 minutes, until lightly browned on the outside.

2 Remove the skillet from the heat and drain off as much oil as possible. Stir in the tarragon and smoked chicken and let the mixture cool completely.

3 Preheat the oven to 425°F/220°C. Brush a cookie sheet or a deep pizza pan with oil.

4 Place the pizza base on the prepared baking sheet and brush with 1 tablespoon of the remaining oil. Spoon the chicken mixture on top and sprinkle with the oregano. Drizzle with the remaining oil and sprinkle with the mozzarella. Bake in the preheated oven for 25–30 minutes, until the cheese is golden and bubbling. Serve immediately.

the ultimate chicken burger

SERVES 4

4 large skinless, boneless chicken breasts

1 large egg white

1 tbsp cornstarch

1 tbsp all-purpose flour

1 egg, beaten

1 cup fresh breadcrumbs

2 tbsp corn oil

to serve

4 burger buns, split

2 beefsteak tomatoes, sliced

lettuce leaves

mayonnaise

1 Place each chicken breast between two sheets of plastic wrap and beat firmly with a meat mallet or rolling pin to flatten the chicken slightly. Beat together the egg white and cornstarch, then brush over the chicken. Cover and let chill in the refrigerator for 30 minutes, then coat in the flour.

2 Place the egg in a shallow dish and the breadcrumbs in a separate shallow dish. Dip the chicken breasts first in the egg mixture, allowing any excess to drip back into the dish, then in the breadcrumbs to coat.

3 Heat a heavy-bottom skillet and add the oil. When hot, add the burgers and cook over medium heat for 6–8 minutes on each side, or until golden and the juices run clear when a sharp knife is inserted into the thickest part of the meat.

4 Serve the burgers in the burger buns with the tomato slices, lettuce and a spoonful of mayonnaise.

Step 1

Step 2

Step 3

bacon-wrapped chicken burgers

SERVES 4

1 lb/450 g fresh ground chicken

1 onion, grated

2 garlic cloves, crushed

⅜ cup pine nuts, toasted

½ cup Gruyère cheese, grated

2 tbsp snipped fresh chives

2 tbsp whole wheat flour

8 lean Canadian bacon slices

1–2 tbsp corn oil

salt and pepper

to serve

4 ciabatta rolls

salad leaves

slices of red onion

mayonnaise

chopped scallions

1 Place the ground chicken, onion, garlic, pine nuts, cheese, chives, and salt and pepper to taste in a food processor. Using the pulse button, blend the mixture together using short sharp bursts. Scrape out onto a board and shape into four equal-size burgers. Coat in the flour, then cover and let chill in the refrigerator for 1 hour.

2 Wrap each burger in two bacon slices, securing in place with a wooden toothpick.

3 Heat a heavy-bottom skillet and add the oil. When hot, add the burgers and cook over medium heat for 5–6 minutes on each side, or until the chicken is cooked through. Remove and discard the toothpicks.

4 Serve the burgers in ciabatta rolls, with salad leaves, onion slices, a spoonful of mayonnaise, and chopped scallions.

chicken & corn empanadas

SERVES 4

14 oz/400 g cooked chicken, diced

14 oz/400 g canned creamed-style corn kernels

1 small onion, finely chopped

8 pimento-stuffed green olives, finely chopped

2 tbsp finely chopped fresh cilantro

1 tsp Tabasco sauce, or to taste

1 tsp ground cinnamon

12 oz/350 g ready-made puff pastry, thawed if frozen

all-purpose flour, for dusting

1 egg, beaten

salt and pepper

1 Preheat the oven to 400°F/200°C. Place the chicken, corn, onion, olives, cilantro, Tabasco, cinnamon, and salt and pepper to taste, in a bowl and mix together.

2 Roll out the pastry on a lightly floured work surface. Using a 6-inch/15-cm saucer as a guide, cut out four rounds.

3 Place an equal quantity of filling on one half of each pastry round. Brush the edge of each round with a little of the beaten egg, fold the pastry over the filling, and press the edges together to seal. Crimp the edges with a fork and prick the tops.

4 Place on a baking sheet, brush with the remaining beaten egg and sprinkle lightly with salt. Bake in the preheated oven for 20 minutes, or until golden brown and hot.

spicy chicken muffins

MAKES 12

½ cup sunflower or peanut oil, plus extra for oiling

2 onions, chopped

3 scallions, chopped

1 small fresh red chile, seeded and finely chopped

3 skinless, boneless chicken thighs, chopped into small pieces

1 tsp paprika

scant 2¼ cups self-rising flour

1 tsp baking powder

2 large eggs

1 tbsp lemon juice

1 tbsp grated lemon rind

½ cup sour cream

½ cup plain yogurt

salt and pepper

1 Preheat the oven to 375°F/190°C. Oil a 12-cup muffin pan with oil. Heat a little of the remaining oil in a skillet, add the onions, scallions, and chile, and cook over low heat, stirring constantly, for 3 minutes. Remove from the heat, lift out the onion mixture, and set aside. Heat a little more of the remaining oil in the skillet, add the chicken and paprika, and cook, stirring, over medium heat for 5 minutes. Remove from the heat and set aside.

2 Sift the flour and baking powder into a large mixing bowl. In a separate bowl, lightly beat the eggs, then stir in the remaining oil and the lemon juice and rind. Pour in the sour cream and the yogurt and mix together. Add the egg mixture to the flour mixture, then gently stir in the onion mixture, and chicken. Season to taste with salt and pepper. Do not overstir the batter—it is fine for it to be a little lumpy.

3 Divide the muffin batter equally among the 12 cups in the prepared muffin pan (it should reach the top) Bake in the preheated oven for 20 minutes, or until risen and golden. Remove the muffins from the oven and serve warm, or transfer to a cooling rack and let cool.

chicken kabobs in a yogurt marinade

SERVES 4

1¼ cups Greek-style yogurt

2 garlic cloves, crushed

juice of ½ lemon

1 tbsp chopped fresh herbs such as oregano, dill, tarragon, or parsley

4 large skinless, boneless chicken breasts

salt and pepper

to serve

cooked rice

lettuce leaves

lemon wedges

1 To make the marinade, put the yogurt, garlic, lemon juice, herbs, and salt and pepper to taste in a large bowl and mix together well.

2 Cut the chicken breasts into 1½-inch/4-cm pieces. Add to the yogurt marinade and toss well together until the chicken pieces are coated. Cover and leave to marinate in the refrigerator for about 1 hour.

3 Preheat the broiler. Thread the chicken pieces onto eight flat, greased, metal kabob skewers or presoaked wooden skewers and place on a greased foil-lined broiler pan.

4 Cook the kabobs under the preheated broiler for about 15 minutes, turning and basting occasionally with the remaining marinade, until lightly browned and cooked through. Serve the kabobs on a bed of rice and lettuce leaves with lemon wedges for squeezing over.

Step 1

Step 2

Step 3

chicken & bacon kabobs

SERVES 4

4 skinless, boneless chicken breasts

1 garlic clove, crushed

2 tbsp tomato paste

4 slices of smoked lean bacon

large handful of fresh basil leaves

vegetable oil, for brushing

salt and pepper

mixed salad, to serve

1 Place each piece of chicken between two sheets of plastic wrap and beat firmly with a rolling pin or meat mallet to flatten the chicken to an even thickness.

2 Combine the garlic and tomato paste and spread the mixture over the chicken. Lay a bacon slice over each, then sprinkle with the basil. Season to taste with salt and pepper.

3 Roll up each piece of chicken firmly, then cut into four thick slices. Thread the slices onto four metal kabob skewers or presoaked wooden skewers to hold the chicken in a spiral shape.

4 Preheat the broiler. Brush the spirals lightly with oil and cook under the preheated broiler, turning once, for about 10 minutes, or until the chicken is cooked through. Serve immediately with salad.

chicken & tomato kabobs

SERVES 4

1 lb 2 oz/500 g skinless, boneless chicken breasts

3 tbsp tomato paste

2 tbsp honey

2 tbsp Worcestershire sauce

1 tbsp chopped fresh rosemary, plus extra sprigs to garnish

9 oz/250 g cherry tomatoes

cooked couscous or rice, to serve

1 Cut the chicken into 1-inch/2.5-cm chunks and place in a large bowl.

2 Combine the tomato paste, honey, Worcestershire sauce, and chopped rosemary in a small bowl. Add to the chicken, stirring to coat evenly.

3 Preheat the broiler. Alternating the chicken pieces and cherry tomatoes, thread them onto eight metal kabob skewers or presoaked wooden skewers.

4 Spoon over any remaining glaze. Cook under the preheated broiler for about 8–10 minutes, turning occasionally, until the chicken is cooked through.

5 Garnish with rosemary sprigs and serve immediately with couscous or rice.

chicken & herb fritters

MAKES 8

1 lb 2 oz/500 g mashed potatoes, with butter added

1⅓ cups cooked chicken, chopped

⅔ cups cooked ham, finely chopped

1 tbsp chopped fresh mixed herbs

2 eggs, lightly beaten, but kept separate

1 tbsp milk

2 cups fresh brown breadcrumbs

oil, for shallow-frying

salt and pepper

mixed salad, to serve

1 In a large bowl, blend the potatoes, chicken, ham, herbs, and one egg. Season to taste with salt and pepper. Shape the mixture into small balls or flat patties.

2 Add the milk to the second egg in a dish. Place the breadcrumbs on a plate. Dip the balls in the egg and milk mixture, allowing any excess to drip back into the dish, then roll in the breadcrumbs, to coat them completely.

3 Heat the oil in a large skillet and cook the fritters until golden brown. Serve immediately with a mixed salad.

spicy chicken stir-fry

SERVES 4

2 tbsp sesame oil

1 garlic clove, chopped

3 scallions sliced, plus extra to garnish

1 tbsp cornstarch

2 tbsp rice wine

4 skinless, boneless chicken breasts, cut into strips

1 tbsp Chinese five-spice powder (available in specialty stores)

1 tbsp grated fresh ginger

½ cup chicken stock

3½ oz/100 g baby corn cobs, sliced

3 cups fresh bean sprouts

1 Heat the oil in a preheated wok or large skillet. Add the garlic and scallions and stir-fry over medium–high heat for 1 minute.

2 In a small bowl, mix together the cornstarch and rice wine, then add the mixture to the wok. Stir-fry for 1 minute, then add the chicken, five-spice powder, ginger and stock, and cook for a further 4 minutes. Add the baby corn and cook for 2 minutes, then add the bean sprouts and cook for a further minute.

3 Remove from the heat, garnish with scallions and serve immediately.

Step 1

Step 1

Step 2

chicken & peanut stir-fry

SERVES 4

2 tbsp peanut oil

1 garlic clove, chopped

3 scallions, sliced

4 skinless, boneless chicken breasts, cut into bite-size chunks

1 tbsp grated fresh ginger

½ tsp chili powder

5½ oz/150 g sugar snap peas

4½ oz/125 g baby corn cobs

2 tbsp smooth peanut butter

1 tbsp light soy sauce

cooked rice, to serve

1 Heat the oil in a preheated wok or large skillet. Add the garlic and scallions and stir-fry over medium–high heat for 1 minute. Add the chicken, ginger, and chili powder and stir-fry for 4 minutes. Add the sugar snap peas and baby corn cobs and cook for 2 minutes.

2 In a bowl, mix together the peanut butter and soy sauce, then add the mixture to the wok. Stir-fry for another minute.

3 Remove from the heat, transfer to serving dishes, and serve immediately with rice.

chinese lemon chicken

SERVES 4

10½ oz/300 g skinless, boneless chicken breasts

finely chopped scallions and finely grated lemon rind, to garnish

marinade

⅔ cup lemon juice

1 tbsp light soy sauce

1 tbsp cornstarch

1 Cut the chicken into bite-size cubes and place in a shallow dish.

2 To make the marinade, mix together the lemon juice and soy sauce in a bowl. Put the cornstarch in another bowl and stir in the lemon and soy mixture to form a paste. Spread over the chicken and let marinate for 15 minutes.

3 Heat a nonstick skillet and add the chicken and marinade. Cook, stirring, for 10–12 minutes, or until the chicken is cooked through. Transfer to serving plates and pour over the sauce. Garnish with scallions and lemon rind and serve immediately.

chicken fried rice

SERVES 4

½ **tbsp sesame oil**

6 shallots, quartered

1 lb/450 g cooked chicken, diced

3 tbsp soy sauce

2 carrots, diced

1 celery stalk, diced

1 red bell pepper, seeded and diced

1½ cups fresh peas

3½ oz/100 g canned corn kernels, drained

3⅔ cups cooked long-grain rice

2 large eggs, scrambled

1 Heat the oil in a large skillet over medium heat. Add the shallots and cook until softened, then add the chicken and 2 tablespoons of the soy sauce and stir-fry for 5–6 minutes.

2 Stir in the carrots, celery, red bell pepper, peas, and corn and stir-fry for an additional 5 minutes. Add the rice and stir thoroughly.

3 Finally, stir in the scrambled eggs and the remaining soy sauce. Serve immediately.

fettuccine with chicken & basil pesto

SERVES 4

2 tbsp vegetable oil

4 skinless, boneless chicken breasts

12 oz/350 g dried fettuccine

salt and pepper

pesto

1⅔ cups shredded fresh basil, plus extra sprigs to garnish

½ cup extra virgin olive oil

3 tbsp pine nuts

3 garlic cloves, crushed

generous pinch of salt

½ cup freshly grated Parmesan cheese

2 tbsp freshly grated Romano cheese

1 To make the pesto, put the shredded basil, olive oil, pine nuts, garlic, and salt in a food processor or blender. Process the ingredients until smooth. Scrape the mixture into a bowl and stir in the cheeses.

2 Heat the vegetable oil in a skillet over medium heat. Cook the chicken breasts, turning once, for 8–10 minutes, or until tender and the juices run clear when a sharp knife is inserted into the thickest part of the meat. Cut into small cubes.

3 Meanwhile, bring a large saucepan of lightly salted water to a boil. Add the pasta, bring back to a boil, and cook for 8–10 minutes, or until tender but still firm to the bite.

4 Drain the pasta and return to the pan. Add the chicken and pesto, then season to taste with pepper. Toss well to mix. Transfer to serving dishes, garnish with basil sprigs and serve immediately.

VARIATION
For a different flavor, try using sun-blush tomato pesto (see page 206) instead of the basil pesto.

3

The Main Event

jerk chicken

SERVES 4

2 red chiles

2 tbsp corn oil, plus extra for brushing

2 garlic cloves, finely chopped

1 tbsp finely chopped onion

1 tbsp finely chopped scallion

1 tbsp white wine vinegar

1 tbsp lime juice

2 tsp raw brown sugar

1 tsp dried thyme

1 tsp ground cinnamon

1 tsp ground allspice

¼ tsp freshly grated nutmeg

4 chicken quarters

salt and pepper

sprigs of fresh cilantro and lime wedges, to garnish

1 Seed and finely chop the chiles, then place them in a small nonmetallic bowl with the oil, garlic, onion, scallion, vinegar, lime juice, raw brown sugar, thyme, cinnamon, allspice, and nutmeg. Season to taste with salt and pepper and mash thoroughly with a fork.

2 Using a sharp knife, make a series of diagonal slashes in the chicken quarters and place them in a large nonmetallic dish. Spoon the jerk seasoning over the chicken, rubbing it well into the slashes. Cover and let marinate in the refrigerator for up to 8 hours.

3 Preheat the broiler. Remove the meat from the marinade, discarding the marinade. Brush with oil and cook under the preheated broiler, turning frequently, for 30–35 minutes, until the juices run clear when a sharp knife is inserted into the thickest part of the meat. Transfer to plates and serve immediately, garnished with sprigs of cilantro and lime wedges.

mustard & honey drumsticks

SERVES 4

8 chicken drumsticks

fresh flat-leaf parsley sprigs, to garnish

glaze

4 tbsp honey

4 tbsp whole grain mustard

4 tbsp white wine vinegar

2 tbsp corn oil

salt and pepper

1 Using a sharp knife, make 2–3 diagonal slashes in the chicken drumsticks and place them in a large nonmetallic dish.

2 Mix together all the ingredients for the glaze, seasoning to taste with salt and pepper. Pour the glaze over the drumsticks, turning until the drumsticks are well coated. Cover with plastic wrap and let marinate in the refrigerator for at least 1 hour.

3 Preheat the broiler. Drain the chicken drumsticks, reserving the marinade. Cook the chicken under the preheated broiler, turning frequently and basting with the reserved marinade, for 25–30 minutes, or until the chicken is tender and the juices run clear when a sharp knife is inserted into the thickest part of the meat. Transfer to serving plates, garnish with parsley sprigs, and serve immediately.

spicy chicken drumsticks

SERVES 4

2 tbsp sunflower oil

8 chicken drumsticks

1 onion, finely chopped

1 tsp chili powder

1 tsp ground coriander

14 oz/400 g canned chopped tomatoes

2 tbsp tomato paste

⅔ cup frozen corn

salt and pepper

mixed bell pepper salad, to serve

1 Heat the oil in a large skillet. Add the chicken drumsticks and cook over medium heat, turning occasionally, until lightly browned. Remove the chicken drumsticks from the pan with a slotted spoon and set aside until required.

2 Add the onion to the pan and cook for 3–4 minutes, until softened, then stir in the chili powder and ground coriander, and cook for a few seconds, stirring briskly so the spices do not burn. Add the tomatoes and the tomato paste and stir well to combine.

3 Return the chicken drumsticks to the pan and simmer gently for 20 minutes, or until the chicken is tender and the juices run clear when a sharp knife is inserted into the thickest part of the meat. Add the corn and cook for another 3–4 minutes. Season to taste with salt and pepper.

4 Serve immediately with a mixed bell pepper salad.

crispy-coated chicken breasts

SERVES 4

1¾ oz/50 g hazelnuts, toasted and ground

3 tbsp dried white or whole wheat breadcrumbs

2 tbsp freshly grated Romano cheese

1 tbsp chopped fresh parsley

4 skinless, boneless chicken breasts

1 egg, beaten

4 tbsp vegetable oil

salt and pepper

salad leaves, to serve

sweet potato wedges

4 large sweet potatoes, peeled and cut into wedges

4 tbsp vegetable oil

1 tsp chili powder

1 Preheat the oven to 400°F/200°C. To make the sweet potato wedges, bring a large pan of water to a boil. Add the potatoes and bring back to a boil and cook for 5 minutes. Drain well. Pour 2 tablespoons of the oil into a large bowl and stir in the chili powder. Add the potatoes and turn in the mixture until coated. Transfer to a cookie sheet, drizzle over the remaining oil, and bake in the preheated oven, turning frequently, for 35–40 minutes, until golden and cooked through.

2 Meanwhile, put the hazelnuts, breadcrumbs, cheese, and parsley into a bowl. Season and mix. Dip the chicken breasts into the beaten egg, allowing the excess to drip back into the dish, then coat in the breadcrumb mixture.

3 Heat the oil in a skillet. Add the chicken and cook over medium heat for 3–4 minutes on each side, until tender and the juices run clear when a sharp knife is inserted into the thickest part of the meat. Lift out and drain on paper towels.

4 Remove the potatoes from the oven, divide among four serving plates, and add a chicken breast to each. Serve immediately with salad leaves.

Step 1

Step 1

Step 3

cheddar-baked chicken

SERVES 4

1 tbsp milk

2 tbsp mustard

1 cup grated cheddar

3 tbsp all-purpose flour

2 tbsp chopped fresh chives

**4 skinless, boneless
chicken breasts**

salad leaves, to serve

1 Preheat the oven to 400°F/200°C. Mix together the milk and mustard in a bowl. In a separate bowl, combine the cheese, flour, and chives.

2 Dip the chicken breasts into the milk and mustard mixture, allowing the excess to drip back into the bowl.

3 Dip the chicken breasts into the cheese mixture, pressing to coat evenly. Place on a baking sheet and spoon any remaining cheese mixture over the top.

4 Bake in the preheated oven for 30–35 minutes, until golden brown and the juices run clear when a sharp knife is inserted into the thickest part of the meat. Serve immediately with salad leaves.

chicken nuggets

SERVES 4

**3 skinless, boneless
chicken breasts**

4 tbsp whole wheat flour

1 tbsp wheat germ

½ tsp ground cumin

½ tsp ground coriander

1 egg, lightly beaten

2 tbsp olive oil

pepper

dipping sauce

**3½ oz/100 g sunblush
tomatoes**

**3½ oz/100 g fresh tomatoes,
peeled, seeded, and
chopped**

2 tbsp mayonnaise

1 Preheat the oven to 375°F/190°C. Cut the chicken breasts into 1½-inch/4-cm chunks. Mix the flour, wheat germ, cumin, coriander, and pepper to taste in a bowl, then divide in half and put on two separate plates. Put the beaten egg on a third plate.

2 Pour the oil into a baking sheet with a rim and heat in the preheated oven. Roll the chicken pieces in one plate of flour, shake to remove any excess, then roll in the egg and in the second plate of flour, again shaking off any excess flour. When all the nuggets are ready, remove the baking sheet from the oven and toss the nuggets in the hot oil. Roast in the oven for 25–30 minutes until cooked through, golden and crisp.

3 Meanwhile, to make the dipping sauce, put both kinds of tomatoes in a blender or food processor and process until smooth. Add the mayonnaise and process again until well combined.

4 Remove the nuggets from the oven and drain on paper towels. Serve immediately with the dipping sauce.

buttermilk fried chicken

SERVES 4

**1 whole chicken
(about 4 lbs/1.8 kg), cut
in 8 serving size pieces**

1 tsp salt

1 tsp black pepper

1 tsp paprika

½ tsp cayenne pepper

½ tsp white pepper

1 tsp poultry seasoning

2 cups buttermilk

peanut oil, for deep-frying

seasoned flour

2 cups all-purpose flour

1 tbsp salt

1 tsp black pepper

1 tsp paprika

¼ tsp cayenne pepper

½ tsp white pepper

1 tsp garlic salt

1 tsp onion powder

1 Place the chicken in a large glass bowl or plastic container. Add all the seasonings, and toss to coat very thoroughly. Pour over the buttermilk. Use tongs to move the chicken pieces around until they are coated. Cover and refrigerate for 6 to 12 hours.

2 Mix together the seasoned flour ingredients in a large baking dish. Drain the chicken pieces in a colander, and toss in the flour until completely coated. Gently shake off excess flour, and transfer to a plate.

3 Heat the oil in a heavy Dutch oven to 350°F/180°C, or until a cube of bread browns in 30 seconds. Carefully add the chicken and fry for 10 minutes. Use tongs or a wire strainer to turn the pieces over, and continue cook for another 8 to 10 minutes approximately, or until the chicken is crisp and golden brown and the juices run clear when a sharp knife is inserted into the thickest part of the meat.

4 Remove to drain on a wire rack for 5 minutes before serving. May be sprinkled with additional salt and/or hot pepper if desired.

thai chicken

SERVES 4

6 garlic cloves, coarsely chopped

1 tsp pepper

8 chicken legs

1 tbsp Thai fish sauce

4 tbsp dark soy sauce

to garnish/serve

fresh ginger cut into matchsticks

fresh cilantro sprigs

finely chopped scallions

cooked rice

1 Put the garlic in a mortar, add the pepper and pound to a paste with a pestle. Using a sharp knife, make 3 to 4 diagonal slashes on both sides of the chicken legs.

2 Spread the garlic paste over the chicken legs and place them in a dish. Add the fish sauce and soy sauce and turn the legs to coat well. Cover with plastic wrap and let marinate in the refrigerator for 2 hours.

3 Preheat the broiler. Drain the chicken legs, setting aside the marinade. Put them on a preheated broiler rack and cook under the broiler, turning and basting frequently with the reserved marinade, for 20 to 25 minutes, or until the chicken is tender and the juices run clear when a sharp knife is inserted into the thickest part of the meat.

4 Transfer the chicken to serving plates and garnish with fresh ginger, cilantro sprigs, and scallions. Serve immediately with rice.

Step 1

Step 1

Step 4

sweet & sour chicken

SERVES 4

4 skinless, boneless chicken breasts

½ cup all-purpose flour

2 tbsp olive oil

2 large garlic cloves, chopped

1 bay leaf

1 tbsp grated fresh ginger

1 tbsp chopped lemongrass

4 tbsp sherry vinegar

5 tbsp rice wine or sherry

1 tbsp honey

1 tsp chili powder

½ cup orange juice

4 tbsp lime juice

salt and pepper

freshly cooked noodles, to serve

wedges of lime, to garnish

1 Season the chicken breasts on both sides with salt and pepper to taste, then roll them in the flour until coated. Heat the oil in a large skillet. Add the garlic and cook, stirring, over medium heat for 1 minute. Add the chicken breasts with the bay leaf, ginger, and lemongrass and cook for 2 minutes on each side.

2 Add the vinegar, rice wine, and honey, bring to a boil, then reduce the heat and simmer, stirring occasionally, for 10 minutes. Add the chili powder, then stir in the orange juice and lime juice. Simmer for another 10 minutes.

3 Using a slotted spoon, lift out the chicken and set aside. Strain and reserve the liquid, discarding the bay leaf, then return the liquid to the pan with the chicken. Simmer for another 15–20 minutes, until the chicken is tender and the juices run clear when a sharp knife is inserted into the thickest part of the meat.

4 Remove from the heat and transfer to serving plates. Serve with freshly cooked noodles and garnish with lime wedges.

chicken pot pies

SERVES 6

1 tbsp olive oil

**8 oz white button
mushrooms, sliced**

1 diced onion

2 cup sliced carrots

1 cup sliced celery

4 cups cold chicken stock

6 tbsps butter

**½ cup all-purpose flour,
plus extra for dusting**

**2 lbs skinless, boneless
chicken breasts, cut in
1-inch/2.5-cm cubes**

1 cup frozen green peas

**1 tsp chopped fresh thyme
leaves or a pinch of dried**

1 lb 8 oz/675 g pie dough

1 egg, beaten

salt and pepper

1 Preheat oven to 400°F/200°C. Heat the oil in a large saucepan and sauté the mushrooms and onions over medium heat until golden. Add the carrots, celery, and 2 cups of chicken stock. Bring to a boil, reduce the heat to low and simmer for 12–15 minutes until the vegetables are almost tender.

2 Meanwhile, melt the butter in a large saucepan over medium heat. Whisk in the flour and cook, stirring, for 4 minutes. Slowly whisk in the remaining stock. Simmer over medium–low heat, stirring, until the mixture thickens. Remove from heat and reserve.

3 Add the vegetables and stock to the sauce and stir to combine. Add the chicken, peas, thyme, salt and pepper. Bring back to a simmer and cook, stirring, for 5 minutes. Taste and adjust the seasoning, adding salt and pepper if needed.

4 Divide the pot pie filling between 6 ramekins or individual ovenproof dishes (fill up to ½ inch/1 cm from the top). Roll out the pie dough on a lightly floured surface and cut out circles 1 inch/2.5 cm larger than the ramekins. Place the dough over the pot pies. Fold the dough over the ramekins to form a rim and pinch to make a crimped edge. Cut a small cross in the center of each crust.

5 Place the ramekins on a baking sheet. Brush the tops with the beaten egg. Bake in the preheated oven for 35–40 minutes, or until pies are golden brown and bubbling. Cool for 15 minutes before serving.

chicken, potato & leek pie

SERVES 4

8 oz/225 g waxy potatoes, cubed

5 tbsp butter, plus 3 tbsp melted

1 skinless, boneless chicken breast, about 6 oz/175 g, cubed

1 leek, sliced

2 cups sliced button mushrooms

2½ tbsp all-purpose flour

1¼ cups milk

1 tbsp whole grain mustard

2 tbsp chopped fresh sage

8 oz/225 g filo dough, thawed if frozen

salt and pepper

1 Preheat the oven to 350°F/180°C. Cook the potato cubes in a pan of boiling water for 5 minutes. Drain and set aside.

2 Melt 5 tablespoons of the butter in a skillet and cook the chicken cubes for 5 minutes or until browned all over.

3 Add the leek and mushrooms and cook, stirring, for 3 minutes. Stir in the flour and cook, stirring constantly, for 1 minute. Gradually stir in the milk and bring to a boil. Add the mustard, sage, and potato cubes, reduce the heat, and simmer for 10 minutes. Season to taste with salt and pepper.

4 Meanwhile, line a deep pie dish with half the sheets of filo dough. Spoon the filling into the dish and cover with one sheet of dough. Brush the dough with a little of the melted butter and lay another sheet on top. Brush this sheet with more melted butter.

5 Cut the remaining filo dough into strips and fold them onto the top of the pie to create a ruffled effect. Brush the strips with the remaining melted butter and cook in the preheated oven for 45 minutes, or until golden brown and crisp. Serve immediately.

broiled chicken with lemon

SERVES 4

4 chicken quarters

juice and grated rind of 2 lemons

4 tbsp olive oil

2 garlic cloves, crushed

2 fresh thyme sprigs, plus extra to garnish

salt and pepper

1 Prick the skin of the chicken quarters all over with a fork. Put the chicken in a dish, add the lemon juice, oil, garlic, thyme, and salt and pepper to taste and mix well. Cover and let marinate in the refrigerator for at least 2 hours.

2 Preheat the broiler. Drain the chicken, reserving the marinade. Put the chicken in a broiler pan and baste with the reserved marinade. Cook under the preheated broiler, turning and basting occasionally, until the chicken is tender and the juices run clear when a sharp knife is inserted into the thickest part of the meat.

3 Serve the chicken immediately, garnished with the grated lemon rind and thyme sprigs

Step 1

Step 1

Step 1

roasted chicken & sweet potatoes

SERVES 4

8 chicken thighs

1 red onion, minced

8 tbsp tomato ketchup

2 tbsp maple syrup

1 tbsp Worcestershire sauce

1 tbsp whole grain mustard

1 garlic clove, minced

3 tbsp olive oil

4 sweet potatoes, peeled and cut into chunks

1 Preheat the oven to 400°F/200°C. Using a sharp knife, make a few slashes in the chicken thighs.

2 Mix together all the remaining ingredients, except the sweet potatoes, in a large bowl. Add the chicken and toss well to coat. Cover with plastic wrap and let marinate in the refrigerator for 20 minutes, then add the sweet potatoes and toss well to coat.

3 Tip the chicken and sweet potatoes into a baking dish and roast in the preheated oven for 40–50 minutes, until well browned. The chicken should be tender and the juices run clear when a sharp knife is inserted into the thickest part of the meat. Serve immediately.

chicken tikka masala

**2 tbsp ghee or vegetable
or peanut oil**

**1 large garlic clove,
finely chopped**

**1 red chile, seeded and
chopped**

2 tsp ground cumin

2 tsp ground paprika

½ tsp salt

**14 oz/400 g canned
chopped tomatoes**

1¼ cups heavy cream

**8 pieces of cooked
tandoori chicken**

pepper

**sprigs of fresh cilantro,
to garnish**

cooked rice, to serve

1 To make the tikka masala, heat the ghee in a large skillet with a lid over medium heat. Add the garlic and chile, and stir-fry for 1 minute. Stir in the cumin, paprika, salt, and pepper to taste and continue stirring for about 30 seconds.

2 Stir the tomatoes with their juice and the cream into the pan. Reduce the heat to low and let the sauce simmer for about 10 minutes, stirring frequently, until it reduces and thickens.

3 Meanwhile, remove all the bones and any skin from the tandoori chicken, then cut the meat into bite-size pieces.

4 Adjust the seasoning of the sauce, if necessary. Add the chicken pieces to the pan, cover, and let simmer for 3–5 minutes, until the chicken is heated through. Garnish with cilantro sprigs and serve immediately with rice.

chicken chow mein

**9 oz/250 g dried medium
egg noodles**

2 tbsp sunflower oil

**9 oz/250 g cooked chicken
breasts, shredded**

**1 garlic clove, finely
chopped**

**1 red bell pepper, seeded
and thinly sliced**

**3½ oz/100 g shiitake
mushrooms, sliced**

6 scallions, sliced

1 cup fresh beansprouts

3 tbsp soy sauce

1 tbsp sesame oil

1 Place the noodles in a large bowl or dish and break them up slightly. Pour enough boiling water over the noodles to cover and let stand. Alternatively, cook according to the packet instructions.

2 Heat the sunflower oil in a large preheated wok. Add the chicken, garlic, bell pepper, mushrooms, scallions, and bean sprouts to the wok and stir-fry for about 5 minutes.

3 Drain the noodles thoroughly. Add the noodles to the wok, toss well, and stir-fry for a further 5 minutes.

4 Drizzle the soy sauce and sesame oil over the chow mein and toss until well combined. Transfer to warmed bowls and serve immediately.

sticky lime chicken

SERVES 4

4 part-boned, skinless chicken breasts, about 5 oz/140 g each

juice and grated rind of 1 lime

1 tbsp honey

1 tbsp olive oil

1 garlic clove, chopped (optional)

1 tbsp chopped fresh thyme, plus extra sprigs to garnish

grated lemon rind, to garnish

pepper

roasted cherry tomatoes and chargrilled zucchini, to serve

1 Preheat the oven to 375°F/190°C. Arrange the chicken breasts in a shallow roasting pan.

2 Put the lime juice and rind, honey, oil, garlic (if using), and thyme in a small bowl and combine thoroughly. Spoon the mixture evenly over the chicken breasts and season to taste with pepper.

3 Roast the chicken in the preheated oven, basting occasionally, for 35–40 minutes, or until the chicken is tender and the juices run clear when a sharp knife is inserted into the thickest part of the meat. As the chicken cooks, the liquid in the pan will thicken to give a sticky coating.

4 Remove from the oven and transfer to plates. Serve immediately with roasted cherry tomatoes, chargrilled zucchini, and garnished with thyme sprigs and grated lemon rind.

Step 1

Step 2

Step 3

paprika chicken with sour cream

SERVES 4

1 tbsp butter

2 tbsp vegetable oil

1 onion, sliced

2 green bell peppers, seeded and chopped

1 tbsp paprika

3 lb 5 oz/1.5 kg chicken thighs and drumsticks

scant 1 cup chicken stock

⅔ cup sour cream

1 tsp all-purpose flour

salt and pepper

1 tbsp snipped fresh dill, to garnish

cooked rice, to serve

1 Heat the butter and 1 tablespoon of the oil in a pan and cook the onion and green bell peppers until softened. Stir in the paprika and season to taste with salt and pepper. Cook, stirring occasionally, for a further 5 minutes.

2 Meanwhile, heat the remaining oil in a lidded flameproof casserole or a heavy-bottom saucepan and cook the chicken portions until browned all over. Add the onion and bell pepper mixture and the stock. Cover tightly and simmer over low heat for 45 minutes. Remove the lid and cook for an additional 15 minutes.

3 Remove the pan from the heat and remove any excess fat from the surface with paper towels. Return to low–medium heat, then gradually stir in the sour cream and then the flour. Simmer gently, stirring, for 3–4 minutes, until thickened. Taste and adjust the seasoning, adding salt and pepper if needed. Garnish with the dill, and serve immediately with rice.

chicken pepperonata

SERVES 4

8 skinless chicken thighs

2 tbsp whole wheat flour

2 tbsp olive oil

1 small onion, sliced thinly

1 garlic clove, crushed

1 each large red, yellow, and green bell peppers, seeded and thinly sliced

14 oz/400 g canned chopped tomatoes

1 tbsp chopped fresh oregano, plus extra to garnish

salt and pepper

crusty whole wheat bread, to serve

1 Toss the chicken thighs in the flour, shaking off the excess.

2 Heat the oil in a large lidded flameproof casserole and cook the chicken quickly until sealed and lightly browned, then remove from the pan.

3 Add the onion to the pan and cook gently until soft. Add the garlic, bell peppers, tomatoes, and oregano, then bring to a boil, stirring.

4 Arrange the chicken over the vegetables and season well with salt and pepper, then cover the pan tightly, reduce the heat, and simmer for 20–25 minutes, or until the chicken is completely tender and the juices run clear when a sharp knife is inserted into the thickest part of the meat.

5 Taste and adjust the seasoning, adding salt and pepper if needed. Garnish with oregano, and serve immediately with crusty whole wheat bread.

mediterranean chicken

SERVES 6

1 tbsp olive oil

6 skinless, boneless chicken breasts

2 cups mozzarella cheese, sliced

3½ cups sliced zucchini

6 large tomatoes, sliced

1 small bunch of fresh basil leaves, torn, plus extra to garnish

pepper

1 Preheat the oven to 400°F/200°C. Cut out six pieces of foil each about 10-inches/25-cm square. Brush the foil squares lightly with the oil and set aside until required.

2 Using a sharp knife, make several slashes in each chicken breast and place the mozzarella between the cuts in the chicken.

3 Divide the zucchini and tomatoes between the pieces of foil, and season with pepper to taste. Scatter the basil over the vegetables in each package.

4 Place the chicken on top of each pile of vegetables, then fold up the foil to enclose the chicken and vegetables, tucking in the ends.

5 Place on a cookie sheet and bake in the preheated oven for about 30 minutes, until the chicken is tender and the juices run clear when a sharp knife is inserted into the thickest part of the meat.

6 Unwrap the foil packages and arrange the chicken and vegetables on serving plates. Garnish with basil leaves and serve immediately.

chicken meatball pasta

SERVES 4

3 tbsp olive oil

1 red onion, chopped

14 oz/400 g skinless, boneless chicken breasts, chopped

1 cup fresh white breadcrumbs

2 tsp dried oregano

1 garlic clove, crushed

14 oz/400 g canned chopped tomatoes

1 tbsp sun-dried tomato paste

8 oz/225 g dried spaghetti or linguine

salt and pepper

Parmesan cheese shavings, to serve

1 Heat 1 tablespoon of the oil in a large skillet and cook half the chopped onion for 5 minutes, until just softened. Let cool.

2 Put the chicken, breadcrumbs, oregano, and cooked onion in a food processor. Season well with salt and pepper and process for 2–3 minutes, until thoroughly combined. Shape into 24 meatballs.

3 Heat the remaining oil in the skillet and cook the meatballs over medium–high heat for 3–4 minutes, until golden brown. Remove and set aside.

4 Add the remaining onion and the garlic to the skillet and cook for 5 minutes. Stir in the tomatoes, sun-dried tomato paste, and 1½ cups water and bring to a boil. Add the meatballs, reduce the heat, and simmer for 20 minutes. Season to taste with salt and pepper.

5 Meanwhile, bring a large pan of lightly salted water to a boil. Add the pasta, bring back to a boil, and cook for 8–10 minutes, until tender but still firm to the bite. Drain well, toss with the meatballs and sauce, and serve immediately with Parmesan cheese shavings.

Step 1

Step 2

Step 5

chicken lasagna

SERVES 4

12 oz/350 g frozen chopped spinach, thawed and drained

½ tsp ground nutmeg

1 lb/450 g lean cooked chicken, diced

4 sheets of no-precook lasagna verde

1½ tbsp cornstarch

scant 2 cups milk

4 tbsp freshly grated Parmesan cheese

salt and pepper

tomato sauce

14 oz/400 g canned chopped tomatoes

1 onion, finely chopped

1 garlic clove, crushed

⅔ cup white wine

3 tbsp tomato paste

1 tsp dried oregano

salt and pepper

1 Preheat the oven to 400°F/200°C. To make the tomato sauce, place the tomatoes in a saucepan and stir in the onion, garlic, wine, tomato paste, and oregano. Bring to a boil, reduce the heat, and simmer for 20 minutes, until thick. Season to taste with salt and pepper.

2 Drain the spinach again and pat dry on paper towels. Arrange the spinach in the base of a rectangular ovenproof dish. Sprinkle with the nutmeg and season to taste.

3 Arrange the diced chicken over the spinach and spoon the tomato sauce over it. Arrange the lasagna sheets over the tomato sauce.

4 Blend the cornstarch with a little of the milk to make a paste. Pour the remaining milk into a pan and stir in the cornstarch paste. Heat gently, stirring constantly, for 2–3 minutes until the sauce thickens. Season to taste with salt and pepper.

5 Spoon the sauce over the lasagna sheets to cover them completely and transfer the dish to a baking sheet. Sprinkle the grated cheese over the sauce and bake in the preheated oven for 25 minutes, until golden brown and bubbling. Serve immediately.

cajun chicken gumbo

1 tbsp sunflower oil

4 chicken thighs

1 small onion, diced

2 celery stalks, diced

1 small green bell pepper, seeded and diced

½ cup long-grain rice

1¼ cups chicken stock, plus extra if needed

1 small red chile, sliced thinly

9 oz/250 g okra

1 tbsp tomato paste

salt and pepper

1 Heat the oil in a wide pan and sauté the chicken until golden. Remove the chicken from the pan using a slotted spoon. Stir in the onion, celery, and green bell pepper and sauté for 1 minute. Pour off any excess fat.

2 Add the rice and sauté, stirring briskly, for another 1 minute. Add the stock and bring to a boil.

3 Add the chile and okra to the pan with the tomato paste. Season to taste with salt and pepper.

4 Return the chicken to the pan and stir. Cover tightly, reduce the heat, and simmer gently for 15 minutes, stirring occasionally and adding a little extra stock if the mixture becomes too dry, or until the rice is tender and the juices run clear when a sharp knife is inserted into the thickest part of the meat. Serve immediately.

sweet chili chicken with creole rice

SERVES 4

8 skinless, boneless chicken thighs, about 3½ oz/100 g each

2 tbsp sweet chili sauce

2 tbsp orange juice

2 garlic cloves, crushed

salt and pepper

creole rice

2½ cups water

1¼ cups long-grain rice

1 tbsp olive oil

1 large red bell pepper, seeded and finely chopped

1 small onion, finely chopped

1 tsp paprika

14 oz/400 g canned mixed beans, drained and rinsed

salt

1 Put the chicken in a shallow, non-metallic bowl. Mix together the chili sauce, orange juice, garlic, and a little salt and pepper in a small bowl and spoon over the chicken. Turn the chicken to coat thoroughly in the marinade. Cover and let marinate in the refrigerator for 1–2 hours.

2 Preheat the oven to 350°F/180°C. Transfer the chicken thighs to a nonstick baking sheet and bake in the preheated oven, turning halfway through, for 25 minutes, or until tender and the juices run clear when a sharp knife is inserted into the thickest part of the meat.

3 Meanwhile, make the rice. Pour the water into a saucepan, add a little salt and bring to the boil. Add the rice and stir well. Cover, then reduce the heat to low and let simmer, undisturbed, for 15 minutes, or until tender and all the water has been absorbed.

4 Meanwhile, heat the oil in a nonstick skillet over medium–high heat. Add the bell pepper and onion, and cook, stirring frequently, for 10–15 minutes, or until the onion is soft and golden, add the paprika for the last 5 minutes of the cooking time. Stir in the beans and cook for an additional minute.

5 Stir the bean mixture into the cooked rice. Transfer to serving plates and top with the chicken. Serve immediately.

chicken, chile & potato stew

SERVES 4

2 tbsp vegetable oil

**1 lb/450 g skinless,
boneless chicken
breasts, cubed**

1 onion, finely chopped

**1 green bell pepper, seeded
and finely chopped**

1 potato, diced

1 sweet potato, diced

**2 garlic cloves, very finely
chopped**

**1–2 fresh green chiles,
seeded and very finely
chopped**

**7 oz/200 g canned chopped
tomatoes**

½ tsp dried oregano

½ tsp salt

½ tsp pepper

**4 tbsp chopped fresh
cilantro**

2 cups chicken stock

1 Heat the oil in a large heavy-bottom pan over medium–high heat. Cook the chicken until lightly browned.

2 Reduce the heat to medium. Add the onion, bell pepper, potato, and sweet potato. Cover and cook, stirring occasionally, for 5 minutes, until the vegetables begin to soften.

3 Add the garlic and chiles. Cook for 1 minute. Stir in the tomatoes, oregano, salt, pepper, and 2 tablespoons of the cilantro. Cook for 1 minute.

4 Pour in the stock. Bring to a boil, then reduce the heat, cover, and simmer over low–medium heat for 15–20 minutes, or until the chicken is cooked through and the vegetables are tender.

5 Transfer to serving dishes and sprinkle over the remaining cilantro. Serve immediately.

VARIATION
Stir in 7 oz/200 g sweetcorn with the tomatoes. For added warmth, stir in ½ teaspoon of ground coriander seeds with the oregano.

4

Food for Friends

coq au vin

SERVES 4

¼ **cup butter**

2 tbsp olive oil

4 lb/1.8 kg chicken pieces

**4 oz/115 g rindless smoked
bacon, cut into strips**

**4 oz/115 g pearl onions,
peeled**

**4 oz/115 g button
mushrooms, halved**

**2 garlic cloves, finely
chopped**

2 tbsp brandy

scant 1 cup red wine

1¼ cups chicken stock

1 bouquet garni

2 tbsp all-purpose flour

salt and pepper

bay leaves, to garnish

1 Melt half the butter with the oil in a large flameproof casserole. Add the chicken and cook over medium heat, stirring, for 8–10 minutes, or until golden brown. Add the bacon, onions, mushrooms, and garlic.

2 Pour in the brandy and set it alight with a match or taper. When the flames have died down, add the wine, stock, and bouquet garni and season to taste with salt and pepper. Bring to a boil, reduce the heat, and simmer gently for 1 hour, or until the chicken is tender and the juices run clear when a sharp knife is inserted into the thickest part of the meat. Meanwhile, make a beurre manié by mashing the remaining butter with the flour in a small bowl.

3 Remove and discard the bouquet garni. Transfer the chicken to a large plate and keep warm. Stir the beurre manié into the casserole, a little at a time. Bring to a boil, return the chicken to the casserole briefly, and serve immediately, garnished with bay leaves.

chicken risotto

SERVES 4

4 tbsp butter

1 onion, chopped

**4½ oz/125 g skinless
chicken breasts, chopped**

12 oz/350 g risotto rice

1 tsp turmeric

1¼ cups white wine

**5 cups hot chicken stock,
plus extra if needed**

**2¾ oz/75 g button
mushrooms, sliced**

**1¾ oz/50 g cashews,
broken in half**

salt and pepper

**shavings of fresh Parmesan
cheese and fresh basil
leaves, to garnish**

1 Melt the butter in a large pan over medium heat. Add the onion and cook, stirring, for 1 minute. Add the chicken and cook, stirring, for an additional 5 minutes.

2 Add the rice and cook, stirring, for 1 minute. Add the turmeric, season with salt and pepper, and mix well. Gradually stir in the wine, then stir in the hot stock, a ladleful at a time, waiting for each ladleful to be absorbed before stirring in the next. Simmer for 20 minutes, stirring from time to time, until the rice is tender and nearly all of the liquid has been absorbed. If necessary, add a little more stock to prevent the risotto from drying out. Stir in the mushrooms and cashews, and cook for another 3 minutes.

3 Remove the risotto from the heat and spoon into warmed serving dishes. Scatter over the Parmesan shavings and basil leaves and serve immediately.

thai green chicken curry

SERVES 4

2 tbsp peanut or vegetable oil

4 scallions, coarsely chopped

2 tbsp green curry paste

3 cups canned coconut milk

1 chicken stock cube

6 skinless, boneless chicken breasts, about 4 oz/115 g each, cut into 1-inch/2.5-cm cubes

large handful of fresh cilantro, chopped

1 tsp salt

cooked rice, to serve

1 Heat the oil in a preheated wok. Add the scallions and stir-fry over medium–high heat for 30 seconds, or until starting to soften.

2 Add the curry paste, coconut milk, and stock cube and bring gently to a boil, stirring occasionally. Add the chicken cubes, half the cilantro, and the salt and stir well. Reduce the heat and simmer gently for 8–10 minutes, or until the chicken is cooked through and tender. Stir in the remaining cilantro. Serve immediately with rice.

chicken kiev

4 oz/115 g butter, softened

3–4 garlic cloves, very finely chopped

1 tbsp chopped fresh parsley

1 tbsp chopped fresh chives

juice and finely grated rind of ½ lemon

8 skinless boneless chicken breasts, about 4 oz/115 g each

⅜ cup all-purpose flour

2 eggs, lightly beaten

1½ cups uncolored dry breadcrumbs

peanut or corn oil, for deep-frying

salt and pepper

cooked green vegetables, to serve

1 Beat the butter in a bowl with the garlic, herbs, lemon juice and rind. Season to taste with salt and pepper. Divide into eight pieces, then shape into cylinders. Wrap in foil and let chill in the refrigerator for about 2 hours or until firm.

2 Place each chicken breast between two sheets of plastic wrap. Pound gently with a meat mallet or rolling pin until evenly thin. Place a butter cylinder on each chicken piece and roll up. Secure with toothpicks.

3 Place the flour, eggs, and breadcrumbs in separate shallow dishes. Dip the chicken rolls into the flour, then into the eggs and, finally, the breadcrumbs. Place on a plate, cover, and let chill in the refrigerator for 1 hour.

4 Heat enough oil for deep-frying in a pan or deep-fryer to 350°F/180°C, or until a cube of bread browns in 30 seconds. Deep-fry the chicken, in batches, for 8–10 minutes, or until cooked through and golden brown. Drain on paper towels. Serve immediately with green vegetables.

Step 1

Step 2

Step 3

tarragon chicken

SERVES 4

4 skinless, boneless chicken breasts, about 6 oz/175 g each

½ cup dry white wine

1–1¼ cups chicken stock

1 garlic clove, finely chopped

1 tbsp dried tarragon

¾ cup heavy cream

1 tbsp chopped fresh tarragon, plus extra sprigs to garnish

salt and pepper

sugar snap peas, to serve

1 Season the chicken with salt and pepper and place in a single layer in a large heavy-bottom skillet. Pour in the wine and enough of the stock just to cover and add the garlic and dried tarragon. Bring to a boil, reduce the heat, and poach gently for 10 minutes, or until the chicken is tender and the juices run clear when a sharp knife is inserted into the thickest part of the meat.

2 Remove the chicken with a slotted spoon, cover, and keep warm. Strain the poaching liquid into a clean saucepan and skim off any fat from the surface. Bring to a boil and cook until reduced by about two thirds.

3 Stir in the cream, return to a boil, and cook until reduced by about half. Stir in the fresh tarragon.

4 Slice the chicken breasts and arrange on warmed plates. Spoon over the sauce, garnish with tarragon sprigs, and serve immediately with sugar snap peas.

chicken & veal roll

SERVES 4

4 oz/115 g ground veal

4 skinless, boneless chicken breast portions, about 4½ oz/125 g each

1 cup cream cheese flavored with garlic and herbs

3 tbsp honey

salt and pepper

fresh sage leaves, to garnish (optional)

1 Put the ground veal in a pan and cook over low–medium heat, stirring frequently, for 5 minutes, until evenly browned and broken up. Season with salt and pepper and let cool.

2 Preheat the oven to 375°F/190°C. Spread out a sheet of plastic wrap and place the chicken portions on top, side by side. Cover with another sheet of plastic wrap and beat gently with a meat mallet or rolling pin until the portions form a continuous sheet about ½ inch/1 cm thick.

3 Remove the chicken from the plastic wrap and spread the cheese over one side of it. Spoon the ground veal evenly over the top. Roll up the chicken from one short side and brush with the honey.

4 Place the chicken roll in a roasting pan and cook for 1 hour in the preheated oven, or until tender and cooked through. Transfer the chicken roll to a cutting board and cut into thin slices. Garnish with sage leaves, if using, and serve immediately.

chicken &
mushroom marsala

SERVES 4

4 thick slices Italian or French bread

2 tbsp olive oil, plus extra for brushing

1 whole garlic clove

4 large boneless chicken breasts, skin on

8 large white mushrooms, sliced

2 tbsps finely minced shallot

2 garlic cloves, minced fine

1½ tbsps flour

1½ cup Marsala wine

2 cups chicken stock

1 tbsp freshly chopped parsley

2 tbsps cold butter, cut in small pieces

salt and pepper

1 Preheat the broiler. Lightly brush the bread slices with olive oil, and toast under the broiler until golden brown on both sides. Rub the rub the whole garlic clove thoroughly over the toasted surface of each slice. Set aside until needed.

2 Season the chicken breasts on both sides generously with salt and pepper. Heat the olive oil in a large skillet over medium-high flame. Place the chicken skin-side down and sear for 5 minutes. Turn over and cook for another 5 minutes, or until the chicken is tender and the juices run clear when a sharp knife is inserted into the thickest part of the meat. Remove from the skillet and set aside.

3 Add the mushrooms, and a pinch of salt to the pan, reduce the heat to medium and cook the mushrooms until they begin to soften and give up their juices. Continue cooking until the liquid evaporates and the mushrooms begin to brown. Add the shallots and garlic and cook, stirring, for 1 minute. Add the flour and cook, stirring, for an additional 2 minutes.

4 Carefully add the Marsala, turn up the heat to high, and cook, stirring, for 2 minutes. While it cooks, scrape the bottom of the pan with a whisk to deglaze any of the caramelized bits. Add the chicken stock and boil until the sauce begins to reduce and thicken slightly.

5 Reduce the heat to very low, return the chicken breasts to the pan and reheat gently. Place a garlic toast on each of four serving plates and top with a chicken breast. Whisk the parsley and butter into the sauce, then spoon the sauce over the top and serve immediately.

chicken with forty cloves of garlic

SERVES 6

**1 chicken, weighing
3 lb 8 oz/1.6 kg**

**3 garlic bulbs, separated
into cloves but unpeeled**

6 fresh thyme sprigs

2 fresh tarragon sprigs

2 bay leaves

1¼ cups dry white wine

salt and pepper

1 Preheat the oven to 350°F/180°C. Season the chicken inside and out with salt and pepper, then truss with kitchen string. Place on a rack in a casserole dish and arrange the garlic and herbs round it.

2 Pour the wine over the chicken and cover with a tight-fitting lid. Cook in the oven for 1½–1¾ hours, or until the chicken is tender and the juices run clear when a sharp knife is inserted into the thickest part of the meat.

3 Transfer the chicken and garlic to a dish and keep warm. Strain the cooking juices into a pitcher. Skim off any fat on the surface of the cooking juices.

4 Carve the chicken and transfer to serving plates with the garlic. Spoon over a little of the cooking juices and serve immediately.

Step 1

Step 1

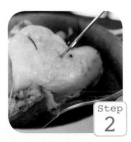

Step 2

chicken fricassée

1 tbsp all-purpose flour

4 skinless, boneless chicken breasts, about 5 oz/140 g each, cut into ¾-inch/2-cm cubes

1 tbsp sunflower or corn oil

8 pearl onions

2 garlic cloves, crushed

1 cup chicken stock

2 carrots, diced

2 celery stalks, diced

2 cups frozen peas

1 yellow bell pepper, seeded and diced

4 oz/115 g white mushrooms, sliced

½ cup lowfat plain yogurt

3 tbsp chopped fresh parsley

salt and pepper

1 Spread out the flour on a dish and season well with salt and pepper. Add the chicken and, using your hands, coat in the flour.

2 Heat the oil in a heavy-bottom pan. Add the onions and garlic, and cook over low heat, stirring occasionally, for 5 minutes. Add the chicken and cook, stirring, for 10 minutes, or until just beginning to color.

3 Gradually stir in the stock, then add the carrots, celery, and peas. Bring to a boil, then reduce the heat, cover, and let simmer for 5 minutes. Add the bell pepper and mushrooms, cover, and let simmer for an additional 10 minutes.

4 Stir in the yogurt and parsley, and season with salt and pepper. Cook for 1–2 minutes, or until heated through, and serve immediately.

chicken in marsala sauce

SERVES 4

2 tbsp all-purpose flour

4 skinless, boneless chicken breasts, sliced lengthwise

3 tbsp olive oil

⅔ cup Marsala wine

2 bay leaves, plus extra to garnish

1 tbsp butter

salt and pepper

cooked rice, to serve

1 Mix the flour, salt, and pepper together on a large plate. Add the chicken and toss to coat.

2 Heat the oil in a skillet over medium heat. Add the chicken and cook for about 4 minutes on both sides, until tender and cooked through. Remove from the skillet and keep warm.

3 Skim most of the fat from the skillet and pour in the Marsala. Add the bay leaves and boil for 1 minute, stirring well, then add the butter with any juices from the chicken and cook until thickened. Remove and discard the bay leaves.

4 Return the chicken to the skillet and heat through. Transfer the chicken to serving plates and spoon over the sauce. Garnish with bay leaves and serve immediately with rice.

chicken with linguine & artichokes

SERVES 4

4 skinless, boneless chicken breasts

juice and finely grated rind of 1 lemon

2 tbsp olive oil

2 garlic cloves, crushed

14 oz/400 g canned artichoke hearts, drained and sliced

9 oz/250 g baby plum tomatoes

10½ oz/300 g dried linguine

salt

chopped fresh flat-leaf parsley and Parmesan cheese, finely grated, to serve

1 Put each chicken breast between two sheets of plastic wrap and pound lightly with a meat mallet or rolling pin to flatten. Put the chicken into a shallow, nonmetallic dish with the lemon juice and rind and 1 tablespoon of the oil and turn to coat in the marinade. Cover and let marinate in the refrigerator for 30 minutes.

2 Heat the remaining oil in a skillet over low heat, add the garlic, and cook, stirring frequently, for 1 minute. Add the artichokes and tomatoes, and cook, stirring occasionally, for 5 minutes. Add about half the marinade from the chicken and cook over medium heat for an additional 5 minutes.

3 Meanwhile, bring a large saucepan of lightly salted water to the boil. Add the pasta, bring back to the boil and cook for 7–9 minutes, or until just tender.

4 Preheat the broiler to high. Remove the chicken from the marinade, discarding the marinade, and arrange on the broiler pan. Cook under the preheated broiler for 5 minutes each side, until the chicken is tender and the juices run clear when a sharp knife is inserted into the thickest part of the meat. Cut the chicken into slices.

5 Drain the pasta and return to the pan, pour the artichoke and tomato mixture into the pan with the sliced, cooked chicken and toss well. Divide among four warmed serving plates and sprinkle over the parsley and cheese. Serve immediately.

creamy chicken with apples

SERVES 4

2 tbsp all-purpose flour

4 chicken legs

1 tbsp olive oil

2 tbsp butter

1 large leek, sliced

⅔ cup chicken stock

⅔ cup apple juice

2 tsp wholegrain mustard

5 tbsp crème fraîche or sour cream

2 red eating apples, cored and thickly sliced

salt and pepper

2 tbsp chopped fresh parsley, to garnish

mashed potatoes, to serve

1 Spread out the flour on a plate and season well with salt and pepper. Toss the chicken legs in the seasoned flour, shaking off any excess. Heat the oil and half the butter in a large deep skillet. Cook the chicken legs over high heat, turning occasionally, for 10 minutes, until golden brown.

2 Add the leeks to the skillet and cook for 1 minute. Pour in the stock and apple juice, then cover, and simmer for 25–30 minutes, or until the chicken is tender and the juices run clear when a sharp knife is inserted into the thickest part of the meat.

3 Using a slotted spoon, remove the chicken from the skillet, cover, and keep warm. Bring the liquid in the pan to a boil and boil rapidly until reduced by one third. Stir in the mustard and crème fraîche, reduce the heat, and simmer for 5 minutes, until the sauce has thickened.

4 Melt the remaining butter in a small skillet and cook the apple slices for 2–3 minutes, until tender and golden. Transfer the chicken and apples to plates, pour the sauce over them, and garnish with parsley. Serve immediately with mashed potatoes.

Step
1

Step
2

Step
4

roast chicken

SERVES 6

**1 chicken, weighing
5 lb/2.25 kg**

4 tbsp butter, softened

**2 tbsp chopped fresh
thyme, plus extra sprigs
to garnish**

1 lemon, quartered

**½ cup white wine, plus
extra if needed**

salt and pepper

1 Preheat the oven to 425°F/220°C. Place the chicken in a roasting pan.

2 Place the butter in a bowl and mix in the chopped thyme and season well with salt and pepper. Butter the chicken all over with the herb butter, inside and out, and place the lemon quarters inside the cavity. Pour the wine over the chicken.

3 Roast the chicken in the center of the preheated oven for 15 minutes. Reduce the temperature to 375°F/190°C and continue to roast for an additional 1¾ hours, basting frequently. Cover with foil if the skin starts to brown too much. If the pan dries out, add a little more wine or water.

4 Test that the chicken is cooked by inserting a sharp knife into the thickest part of the meat and making sure the juices run clear. Remove from the oven.

5 Remove the chicken from the roasting pan and place on a warmed serving plate. Cover with foil and let rest for 10 minutes before carving.

6 Place the roasting pan on top of the stove and heat the pan juices gently over low heat, until they have reduced and are thick and glossy. Serve the chicken with the pan juices and garnish with the thyme sprigs.

pan-fried chicken with golden sauce

SERVES 4

2 mangoes

14 oz/400 g canned apricots in juice

4 tbsp unsalted butter

4 skinless, boneless chicken breasts, about 6 oz/175 g each

pepper

cooked new potatoes sprinkled with snipped chives, to serve

1 Using a sharp knife, slice off the sides of the mangoes as close to the pits as possible. Cut through the flesh in the half shells in a criss-cross pattern, turn inside out, and cut off the flesh. Cut off any remaining flesh from the pits. Place in a food processor.

2 Drain the apricots, setting aside about 1 cup of the can juice. Put the apricots and reserved juice into the food processor with the mangoes and process until smooth. Pour the sauce into a small pan.

3 Melt the butter in a large heavy-bottom skillet. Add the chicken and cook over low–medium heat, turning occasionally, for 15 minutes, until the chicken is tender and the juices run clear when a sharp knife is inserted into the thickest part of the meat.

4 Meanwhile, place the pan of sauce over low heat to warm through, but do not boil.

5 Slice the chicken and arrange on warmed serving plates. Spoon the sauce over the chicken and sprinkle with pepper to taste. Serve immediately with new potatoes.

chicken pinwheels with bleu cheese

SERVES 4

2 tbsp pine nuts, lightly toasted

2 tbsp chopped fresh parsley

2 tbsp chopped fresh thyme

1 garlic clove, chopped

1 tbsp grated lemon zest

4 skinless, boneless chicken breasts

9 oz/250 g bleu cheese, crumbled

salt and pepper

mixed salad leaves, to serve

lemon slices and sprigs of fresh flat-leaf parsley, to garnish

1 Put the pine nuts into a food processor with the parsley, thyme, garlic, and lemon zest. Season with salt and pepper.

2 Put each chicken breast between two pieces of plastic wrap and pound lightly with a meat mallet or rolling pin to flatten them. Spread them on one side with the pine nut mixture, then top with the cheese. Roll them up from one short end to the other, so that the filling is enclosed. Wrap the rolls individually in foil and seal well. Transfer into a steamer, or a metal colander placed over a pan of boiling water, cover tightly, and steam for 10–12 minutes, or until cooked through.

3 Arrange the salad leaves on a large serving platter. Remove the chicken from the heat, discard the foil, and cut the chicken rolls into slices. Arrange the slices over the lettuce leaves. Garnish with slices of lemon and sprigs of parsley, and serve immediately.

winter pot-roast chicken

SERVES 4

2 tbsp sunflower oil

2 tbsp butter

1 chicken, weighing 3 lb/1.3 kg

1½ cups diced parsnips

1½ cups diced rutabaga

1½ cups diced carrots

6 shallots, halved

2 cups chicken stock

3 tbsp pearl barley

1 bouquet garni

salt and pepper

fresh thyme sprigs, to garnish

1 Preheat the oven to 325°F/160°C. Heat 1 tablespoon of the oil and the butter in a large deep skillet. Season the chicken well with salt and pepper and cook in the hot fat, turning, for 7–8 minutes, until lightly browned. Transfer to a large casserole.

2 Add the remaining oil to the skillet and stir in the diced vegetables and shallots. Cook over medium–high heat, stirring, for 10 minutes. Add the stock and pearl barley, then bring to a boil. Reduce the heat, simmer for 5 minutes, then transfer to the casserole. Add the bouquet garni and season to taste with salt and pepper.

3 Cover and cook in the preheated oven for 1¼ hours. Uncover the casserole and cook for an additional 20 minutes, until all the vegetables are tender, the chicken is golden, and the juices run clear when a sharp knife is inserted into the thickest part of the meat. Garnish with thyme sprigs and serve immediately.

Step 1

Step 1

Step 2

harissa
chicken with
chickpea mash

SERVES 4

**4 skinless chicken breasts,
about 5 oz/140 g each**

1 tbsp olive oil

8 tsp harissa (chili) paste

salt and pepper

chickpea mash

2 tbsp olive oil

2–3 garlic cloves, crushed

**14 oz/400 g canned
chickpeas, drained and
rinsed**

4 tbsp milk

**3 tbsp chopped fresh
cilantro, plus extra to
garnish**

salt and pepper

1 Make a few shallow slashes in each chicken breast. Place the chicken in a dish, brush with the olive oil, and coat both sides of each breast with the harissa paste. Season well with salt and pepper, cover, and let marinate in the refrigerator for 30 minutes.

2 Preheat the oven to 425°F/220°C. Transfer the chicken breasts to a roasting pan and roast for about 20–30 minutes, until they are cooked through and the juices run clear when a sharp knife is inserted into the thickest part of the meat.

3 Meanwhile, make the chickpea mash. Heat the oil in a pan and gently fry the garlic for 1 minute, then add the chickpeas and milk, and heat through for a few minutes. Transfer to a blender or food processor and purée until smooth. Season to taste with salt and pepper and stir in the fresh cilantro.

4 To serve, divide the chickpea mash among four serving plates, top each one with a sliced chicken breast, garnish with cilantro, and serve immediately.

chicken with chickpeas

SERVES 4

1 tbsp olive oil

1 onion, cut into small wedges

2–4 garlic cloves, sliced

1 lb/450 g skinless, boneless chicken breasts, diced

1 tsp ground cumin

2 cinnamon sticks, lightly bruised

1 tbsp whole wheat flour

8 oz/225 g eggplant, diced

1 red bell pepper, seeded and chopped

3 oz/85 g button mushrooms, sliced

1 tbsp tomato paste

2½ cups chicken stock

10 oz/280 g canned chickpeas, drained and rinsed

⅓ cup ready-to-eat dried apricots, chopped

salt and pepper

fresh cilantro leaves, to garnish

1 Heat the oil in a large pan over medium heat, add the onion and garlic and cook for 3 minutes, stirring frequently. Add the chicken and cook, stirring constantly, for an additional 5 minutes, or until sealed on all sides. Add the cumin and cinnamon sticks to the pan halfway through sealing the chicken.

2 Sprinkle in the flour and cook, stirring constantly, for 2 minutes.

3 Add the eggplant, red bell pepper, and mushrooms, and cook for an additional 2 minutes, stirring constantly.

4 Blend the tomato paste with the stock, stir into the pan, and bring to a boil. Reduce the heat and add the chickpeas and apricots. Cover and let simmer for 15–20 minutes, or until the chicken is tender and cooked through.

5 Season to taste with salt and pepper. Garnish with cilantro leaves and serve immediately.

chicken casserole with a herb crust

SERVES 4

4 chicken legs

2 tbsp all-purpose flour

1 tbsp olive oil

1 tbsp butter

1 onion, chopped

3 garlic cloves, sliced

4 parsnips, cut into large chunks

1 cup dry white wine

3½ cups chicken stock

3 leeks, white parts only, sliced

3 oz/85 g prunes, halved (optional)

1 tbsp mustard

1 bouquet garni

3½ oz/100 g fresh breadcrumbs

3 oz/85 g feta cheese, crumbled

2 oz/55 g mixed fresh tarragon and flat-leaf parsley, chopped

salt and pepper

1 Preheat the oven to 350°F/180°C. Toss the chicken legs in the flour, shaking off any excess. Melt the oil with the butter in a flameproof casserole. Add the chicken and fry, turning occasionally, until golden brown all over. Remove with a slotted spoon and keep warm.

2 Add the onion, garlic, and parsnips to the casserole and cook until slightly browned. Add the wine, stock, leeks, prunes, if using, mustard, and bouquet garni, and season with salt and pepper to taste.

3 Return the chicken to the casserole, cover, and cook in the oven for 1 hour or until the chicken is tender and the juices run clear when a sharp knife is inserted into the thickest part of the meat. Mix the breadcrumbs, cheese, and herbs together.

4 Remove the casserole from the oven and increase the oven temperature to 400°F/200°C.

5 Sprinkle the casserole with the breadcrumb mixture and return to the oven for 10 minutes, uncovered, until the crust starts to brown slightly. Remove from the oven and serve immediately.

chicken with saffron mash

SERVES 4

**1 lb 4 oz/550 g mealy
potatoes, cut into chunks**

**1 garlic clove, peeled but
left whole**

**1 tsp saffron threads,
crushed**

**5 cups chicken or
vegetable stock**

**4 skinless, boneless
chicken breasts**

2 tbsp olive oil

1 tbsp lemon juice

**1 tbsp chopped fresh
thyme, plus extra sprigs
to garnish**

**1 tbsp chopped fresh
cilantro**

**1 tbsp coriander seeds,
crushed**

⅓ cup hot milk

salt and pepper

1 Put the potatoes, garlic, and saffron in a large heavy-bottom pan, add the stock and bring to a boil. Reduce the heat, cover, and let simmer for 20 minutes, or until tender.

2 Meanwhile, brush the chicken breasts all over with half the olive oil and all of the lemon juice. Sprinkle with the fresh thyme, cilantro, and the crushed coriander seeds. Heat a grill pan, add the chicken and cook over medium–high heat for 5 minutes on each side, or until the chicken is tender and the juices run clear when the meat is pierced with the tip of a sharp knife. Alternatively, cook the chicken breasts under a preheated medium–hot broiler for 5 minutes on each side, or until cooked through.

3 Drain the potatoes and return them to the pan. Add the remaining olive oil and the milk, season to taste with salt and pepper and mash until smooth. Divide the saffron mash among four large, warmed serving plates, top with a piece of chicken, and garnish with thyme sprigs. Serve immediately.

Step
2

Step
3

Step
3

chicken cacciatora

SERVES 4

1 roasting chicken, weighing 3 lb 5 oz/ 1.5 kg, cut into 6 or 8 pieces

1 cup all-purpose flour

3 tbsp olive oil

⅔ cup dry white wine

1 green bell pepper, seeded and sliced

1 red bell pepper, seeded and sliced

1 carrot, finely chopped

1 celery stalk, finely chopped

1 garlic clove, crushed

7 oz/200 g canned chopped tomatoes

salt and pepper

fresh flat-leaf parsley sprigs, to garnish

1 Lightly dust the chicken pieces with seasoned flour. Heat the oil in a large skillet. Add the chicken and fry over a medium heat until browned all over; remove from the pan and set aside.

2 Drain off all but 2 tablespoons of the fat in the pan. Add the wine and simmer, stirring, for a few minutes. Stir in the bell peppers, carrot, celery, and garlic and season with salt and pepper to taste. Return the chicken to the pan and simmer for about 15 minutes.

3 Add the tomatoes to the pan. Cover and simmer for 30 minutes, stirring often, until the chicken is tender and the juices run clear when a sharp knife is inserted into the thickest part of the meat.

4 Taste and adjust the seasoning, adding salt and pepper if needed. Garnish with parsley sprigs and serve immediately.

chicken in white wine

SERVES 4

¼ cup butter

2 tbsp olive oil

2 thick, rindless, lean bacon strips, chopped

4 oz/115 g pearl onions

1 garlic clove, finely chopped

4 lb/1.8 kg chicken pieces

1¾ cups dry white wine

1¼ cups chicken stock

1 bouquet garni

4 oz/115 g button mushrooms

2½ tbsp all-purpose flour

salt and pepper

chopped fresh mixed herbs, to garnish

1 Preheat the oven to 325°F/160°C. Melt half the butter with the oil in a flameproof casserole. Add the bacon and cook over medium heat, stirring, for 5–10 minutes, or until golden brown. Transfer the bacon to a large plate.

2 Add the onions and garlic to the casserole and cook over low heat, stirring occasionally, for 10 minutes, or until golden. Transfer to the plate. Add the chicken and cook over medium heat, stirring constantly, for 8–10 minutes, or until golden. Transfer to the plate.

3 Drain off any excess fat from the casserole. Stir in the wine and stock, then bring to a boil, scraping any sediment off the bottom. Add the bouquet garni and season to taste with salt and pepper. Return the bacon, onions, and chicken to the casserole. Cover and cook in the preheated oven for 1 hour. Add the mushrooms, re-cover, return to the oven, and cook for a further 15 minutes, or until the chicken is tender and the juices run clear when a sharp knife is inserted into the thickest part of the meat. Meanwhile, make a beurre manié by mashing the remaining butter with the flour in a small bowl.

4 Remove the casserole from the oven and set over medium heat. Remove and discard the bouquet garni. Stir the beurre manié into the casserole, a little at a time. Bring to a boil, stirring constantly. Garnish with mixed herbs and serve immediately.

buttered chicken rolls

4 tbsp butter

4 shallots, finely chopped

**10½ oz/300 g frozen
spinach, thawed**

**1 lb/450 g bleu cheese,
crumbled**

1 egg, lightly beaten

**1 tbsp snipped
fresh chives, plus extra
to garnish**

**1 tbsp chopped
fresh oregano**

**4 large, skinless, boneless
chicken breasts**

8 slices of prosciutto

salt and pepper

**baby spinach leaves,
to serve**

1 Melt half of the butter in a skillet over medium heat. Add the shallots and cook, stirring, for 4 minutes. Remove from the heat and let cool for 10 minutes.

2 Preheat the oven to 350°F/180°C. Using your hands, squeeze out as much moisture from the spinach as possible. Transfer the spinach into a large bowl, add the shallots, cheese, egg, herbs, and seasoning. Mix together well.

3 Halve each chicken breast, put between two pieces of plastic wrap, and pound lightly with a meat mallet or rolling pin to flatten them. Spoon some cheese mixture into the center of each piece, then roll them up. Wrap each roll in a slice of prosciutto and secure with a toothpick. Transfer to an ovenproof dish and dot with the remaining butter. Bake in the preheated oven for 30 minutes until golden and cooked through.

4 Divide the baby spinach leaves among four serving plates. Remove the chicken from the oven and place two chicken rolls on each bed of spinach. Garnish with chives and serve immediately.

roasted chicken with sun-blush tomato pesto

SERVES 4

4 skinless, boneless chicken breasts, about 7 oz/200 g each

1 tbsp olive oil

mixed salad, to serve

sun-blush tomato pesto

4½ oz/125 g sun-blush tomatoes in oil (drained weight), chopped

2 garlic cloves, crushed

4 tbsp pine nuts, lightly toasted, plus extra for sprinkling

⅔ cup extra virgin olive oil

1 Preheat the oven to 400°F/200°C. To make the pesto, put the sun-blush tomatoes, garlic, pine nuts, and oil into a food processor and process to a coarse paste.

2 Arrange the chicken in a large ovenproof dish or roasting pan. Brush each breast with the oil, then place a tablespoon of pesto over each breast. Using the back of a spoon, spread the pesto so that it covers the top of each breast.

3 Roast the chicken in the preheated oven for 30 minutes, or until tender and the juices run clear when a sharp knife is inserted into the thickest part of the meat.

4 Transfer the chicken to serving plates, sprinkle with the pine nuts and serve immediately with a mixed salad.

VARIATION

For a version with red bell pepper and chile pesto, make the pesto with 2 skinned and cooked red bell peppers and 2 mild chile peppers, replacing all but 1¾ oz/50 g of the sun-blush tomatoes.